In the Mission Field

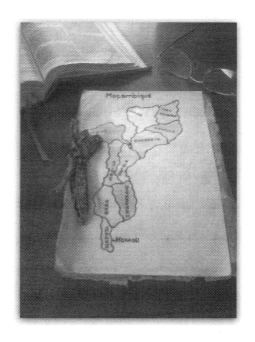

RALPH W.J. SEDRAS

WESTBOW
PRESS
A DIVISION OF THOMAS NELSON
& ZONDERVAN

WestBow Press books may be ordered through booksellers or by contacting:

WestBow Press
A Division of Thomas Nelson & Zondervan
1663 Liberty Drive
Bloomington, IN 47403
www.westbowpress.com
1 (866) 928-1240

Because of the dynamic nature of the Internet, any web addresses or links contained in this book may have changed since publication and may no longer be valid. The views expressed in this work are solely those of the author and do not necessarily reflect the views of the publisher, and the publisher hereby disclaims any responsibility for them.

Any people depicted in stock imagery provided by Thinkstock are models, and such images are being used for illustrative purposes only.
Certain stock imagery © Thinkstock.

ISBN: 978-1-4908-5534-9 (sc)
ISBN: 978-1-4908-5533-2 (e)

Printed in the United States of America.

WestBow Press rev. date: 12/29/2014

CONTENTS

Dedication vii

Foreword.. ix

Acknowledgements xi

1.   Simáo, Ntombiyenkosi Mucache and the Mission Station 1

2.   The Night the Angel of the Lord visited me 2

3.   The Voice, the Vision 3

4.   My Reason for this Mission Trip... 5

5.   God's Supply 7

6.   The Manzinis and Kobus 8

7.   Getting Across the Border – Monday, 02 August 10

8.   Getting to Know More and Little Things to Do – Tuesday, 03 August 16

9.   Realising the Importance of Early Morning Quiet Time – Wednesday, 04 August ...18

10. Using the Jig-Saw – Thursday, 05 August 21

11. The Spider and the Wild Boar – Friday, 06 August 23

12. The Two Sets of Visitors – Saturday, 07 August 28

13. The Message – Sunday, 08 August 30

14. The Trudge to Maputo – Monday, 09 August....................................... 34

15. The Garden Patch – Tuesday, 10 August 36

16. Home Cell in the Jungle – Wednesday, 11 August 38

17. Repairing the Jig-Saw – Thursday, 12 August 41

Images 43

18. The Day I Woke Up With a Splitting Headache – Friday, 13 August 46

19. Feeling Good and on Top of the World Again – Saturday, 14 August 48

20. Relaxing at the Beach after Church – Sunday, 15 August 50

21. The Start of the New Week – Monday, 16 August 55

22. The Bat and I – Tuesday, 17 August 57

23. The Holy Spirit and the Rain – Wednesday, 18 August 60

24. The Children and the Roof – Thursday, 19 August 63

25. The Paper Maché Frames and Laying on of Hands – Friday, 20 August 65

26. Phoning Theresa my wife – Saturday, 21 August 68

27. My Last Week At "Igreja Communitaria de Moçambique" 71

28. Fernando and Me – Monday, 23 August 74

29. Reality- The Sobering Effect – Tuesday, 24 August 77

30. The Visitors – Wednesday, 25 August 81

31. The Rope Ladder – Thursday, 26 August 83

32. Rain and Becoming a Grandfather – Friday, 27 August 88

33. The Birthday – Saturday, 28 August 90

34. The Moment in My Life I Would Never Forget – Sunday, 29 August 93

The Poem 97

Epilogue 99

DEDICATION

This book is dedicated to a dear friend, Ntombiyenkosi (Annette) Mucache, who first became a part of my life and later also that of my family, as a result of our mutual interest in missions.

She was a woman passionate about the calling the Lord, God had laid upon her shoulders. A dedicated, faithful, loving, compassionate, God fearing, woman of strength, she received much from the Lord in dealing with people and their needs.

She was mother to many a child and numerous adults too. No one can refute the fact that she was chosen by God to be an influence wherever she went.

God was always first in her life, then her family and then the needs of others. (Proverbs 31:20)

Ntombi was tragically taken from us in a motor vehicle accident on 17 December 2011 as she was returning home to Moçambique from Cape Town.

We mourn the loss of this courageous woman.

Woman of God, we salute you!

Ntombiyenkosi (Annette) Mucache

FOREWORD

I believe that the LORD laid it on my heart to write this book for someone out there who has a desire to go into the mission field. I went to Moçambique knowing that the LORD, MY DELIVERER had sent me on this mission trip which happened during the month of August 2004. I had no fear of what was to be, because I knew that HE, my DADDY loved me and that it was HE who was sending me.

ACKNOWLEDGEMENTS

I would like to thank the following people without whom this book would not have been completed:

My son, Jaime, friends of the family, Runelda Adams, Jéan, Cindy-Jane Nayger and my sister, Irma Jacobs who did all of the typing as I am completely computer illiterate! Thanks everyone for your sterling efforts.

A special thanks to my wife, Theresa for her invaluable input and assistance with getting the manuscript into the hands of the publishers.

CHAPTER 1

SIMÁO, NTOMBIYENKOSI MUCACHE AND THE MISSION STATION

I was a parent of one of the young adults (Jaime) in May 2004, who was part of a group named "LATREUO" which translated means "slave unto GOD". They were a group of young adults who had given up a year of their lives to serve the LORD. Suzy Abrahams, their leader was one of the pastors at the church we attend (Lighthouse Christian Centre, Parow). She had been called by GOD to missions and had embarked on this trip to Moçambique to a wonderful couple Simáo and Ntombiyenkosi Mucache. They run an orphanage of ± forty to fifty children ranging in age from as young as two years to their late teens. Some of the children do not even know who their parents are.

Little children had been found wandering around in the bush, not knowing which way to turn or go, hungry and crying. When these children saw an adult they ultimately stretched out their arms, looking for love or for someone to just comfort and hold them in their arms. There are older boys and girls who do not want to go home because of circumstances at their homes. They prefer to live away from their parents and to live with strangers who give them love, understanding and counselling.

Simáo and Ntombiyenkosi became parents, mom and dad to these children who in turn love and respect their new found parents. It is so wonderful to see how obedient they are and how they listen when spoken to.

CHAPTER 2

THE NIGHT THE ANGEL OF THE LORD VISITED ME

All arrangements had been made. We were a group of twenty-five consisting of seven adults and eighteen Latreuo members. We travelled with the church's kombi and one of our Pastor's kombi. I do not want to go into detail about this trip, but just to let you know how I travelled to Moçambique.

While we were there, this particular night was the last Tuesday night of a three week trip. I was in bed sharing a bungalow with two of the adults. That night to me it felt as if all night long I was grappling and debating with some super being, like an angel. There was a moment when I thought "when am I ever going to sleep". When I woke up the next morning there was one clear thought in my mind, I must stay behind for another four days and possibly one or two of Latreuo's boys with me.

I spoke to my wife, Theresa who was one of the adults on this trip. I insisted that I wanted to know from her first whether she would agree to me staying behind. Please note that I did not want her permission but her assurance that she would be happy that I stay, seeing how the angel of the LORD had been with me all night. Well her answer was "have you spoken to Suzy, Simáo and Ntombiyenkosi"? I was overjoyed and felt as if I was on top of the world. Suzy was next and her answer "Well if the LORD has spoken to you and you are ok with it then who am I to say no!", I now went to Simáo and Ntombi who were so thrilled that they agreed.

During this last week of our stay, Pastor Peter, his wife Charlotte and their boys arrived. You will see how they fitted into GOD`S plan. It was now Thursday and time for the team's departure to Cape Town. I said my goodbyes to my wife and son and the rest of the team. Not one of them tried to persuade me to come with them; they knew it was GOD`S calling on my life.

CHAPTER 3

THE VOICE, THE VISION

Arrangements had been made for Simáo to get me onto a bus back to Johannesburg and on to Cape Town after my extra four days' stay. Suzy and Theresa found out what it would cost when they arrived in Johannesburg, no one had realised what the cost would be and it became clear that this whole exercise would be too costly for the short time that I would be staying there.

That Friday I fixed broken doors, hinges and other little things I could find to do. In the meantime it was decided by all the parties involved that I would be coming back with Pastor Peter on Saturday, I had no choice. I was disappointed but what could I do, there just were not enough finances.

The Saturday morning came. We had packed the night before and we were all on Simáo's bakkie, Charlotte with their son Zachari-Paul who was on her lap, sat next to Simáo in the front. Peter, Asher, David and I were on the back. We were pointing out interesting sites, trees or an unusual object along the road. We did not see any animals, Simáo had told us that animals were very scarce in the area as during the war all cattle and wild animals were caught and slaughtered for their meat.

As we were driving along we all became quiet and very solemn. Each one lost in his own thoughts. David went to stand with Peter and Asher behind the cab. All of a sudden everything around me was very quiet and I saw the sky opening before my very eyes, the clouds parted and the heavens were displayed before me in all its splendour, I knew something big was going to happen. I then found myself asking GOD. "LORD why the exercise?" The answer came immediately in a loud booming voice almost like thunder "*IT WAS YOUR OBEDIENCE THAT WAS REQUIRED*".

Immediately the vision was gone and I realised that I had been taken away in the spirit and brought back to the bakkie. The amazement of it all was that not one of the others had seen or experienced this wonderful moment in my life out in this beautiful landscaped area.

People, brothers and sisters in the LORD be obedient to the voice of GOD when HE speaks to you. Have faith, believe in HIM and HE will get you where HE wants you to be.

CHAPTER 4

MY REASON FOR THIS MISSION TRIP

What I had seen as a requirement at the mission station was a big need. In spite of having all the jungle, trees, a river, even the sea which was a twenty minute walk from where they were there was an acute lack. There was no playground or any such facility for the children. I felt such a loss for these children. Here in Cape Town we have Parks, Jungle-Jims and Sports facilities so freely available to all people. Yet we as people don't make time for these facilities. All children need to have these facilities made freely available to them.

GOD had spoken to me, I knew I had to go back to build a nice big Jungle-Jim and proper swings for the children. Ntombi had told me that she and Simáo were coming to Cape Town at the end of June to visit a friend and attend his wedding. By the time they came down for the wedding I knew what I had to do.

I spoke to Simáo and Ntombi and she told me she had already bought seats and chains to make swings but had no one to assemble it for them. We both looked at each other and we knew that GOD had set everything in motion already. I found out that August would be the best time to come to Moçambique. They told me that I should come with my luggage only and not worry about anything else. I then asked my wife, Theresa to find out costs of travelling by bus and how many buses I would have to take to reach them in Moçambique. We found the Greyhound bus to be the most suitable from Cape Town station to Johannesburg station. From Johannesburg I travelled on the City to City bus to a place called Manguzi in Kwa Zulu Natal. On arriving there I would be about twenty kilometres from the Cozy Bay border post.

Our GOD is a good GOD and HIS timing and planning is way beyond what we could possibly understand or comprehend.

A few years previously, a group of pastors from the church I attend (Lighthouse Christian Centre, Parow) had decided to go on an outreach trip. I do not know how many were in this group but there they met the pastor in that area, pastor Manzini, who was to host them.

Simáo and Pastor Manzini had been friends for some time and so between the two of them they sorted me out. Pastor Manzini would pick me up and I would stay with him for the weekend and cross the border on Monday.

CHAPTER 5

GOD'S SUPPLY

The time for my departure was drawing near, and I had no finances to get me where GOD wanted me.

It was now two weeks before my departure and I still did not have a cent towards my fare for the trip. Suddenly, things started happening. My mother, bless her, who departed from this world a year after this trip and a dear sister in the church, one of my home cell members, another couple whom we came to know since joining the church and the youth leader at that time, then there was also a member of one of our sister churches and last but not least, one of the dance leaders, all contributed towards my expenses.

I now had enough money to cover all my expenses, enough to leave some with Theresa and enough to bless Simáo and Ntombi with. "GOD is good". I am sharing this so that anyone who feels the need to go on a mission trip but feels he or she is not by the means must have faith in GOD. He won't send you and then leave you to fend for yourself. He will supply all your needs and more. Praise the LORD! This is a special chapter in my life, if it had not been for the LORD I would never have made this trip.

CHAPTER 6

THE MANZINIS AND KOBUS

The day of my departure to Moçambique was upon me, Thursday 27 July 2004 at 18h00 by Greyhound bus from Cape Town station as far as Johannesburg Park station. There was a phone call from Simáo enquiring about my departure, he sounded a bit anxious. I asked whether there was anything wrong but he said that everything was alright and I must go well.

I had a pleasant trip on the bus with reclining seats, DVD player and plenty of stoppages for bathroom facilities, leg stretching or something to eat along the road. There was also a built-in toilet on the bus for any emergency. We arrived the next day Friday at 13h00 the afternoon. I had a long wait till 20h00 that night to catch the City to City bus to Manguzi. This bus was a far cry from the Greyhound bus nonetheless I had to make the most of it. I managed to secure a place at the window so I could at least sleep against the body of the bus. I felt sorry for the guy next to me because he had to sit upright and sleep as best as he could. We had one stop at Ermelo at a fishery with bathroom facilities, a bit crude but we had no choice.

We arrived at Manguzi, Saturday, the next morning at 7.00am. I phoned pastor Manzini as pre-arranged. When he arrived there were hand-shakes, hugs and laughter. I had met him on the June trip with Suzy as some of the team stayed over at his church. I then heard that Simáo's vehicle had broken down and they were going to trust the LORD and see how they could get me across the border and to the mission station.

I would like to add that by this time the person reading this book should realise that a mission trip is all about trusting GOD. I had a good weekend with pastor Manzini and his family. I stayed in one of the bedrooms and was served as if I was a king. Their daughter would kneel before me with my food on a tray as was their custom.

In June when I was in Moçambique with Suzy, although she was our pastor she was also a personal family friend, I saw that they were building a church hall and also their existing church had no name. I made arrangements for the wording and the design they wanted and made them a sign board. On that same trip I made arrangements for a sign at the mission station as well, as I am a sign writer by trade.

Danie Koen one of our missionaries who undertook a missionary trip annually, took both signs up with him on his trip to Simáo and delivered it. He also helped erect the missions sign at a strategic point where one could see it clearly from the road.

Sunday morning, the 1st August, pastor Manzini asked me to present the signboard officially to the church and bless the congregation before we left to go to the dedication of a new Anglican church which had been built for the local people of that area. After all their praying, holy communion, singing and celebrating we went over to the hall to have lunch. GOD had even set up for me to meet Kobus van Schalkwyk, a Dutch Reformed Minister, who after hearing about my predicament, being stranded in Kwa Zulu Natal at the Manzinis, offered to take me across the border on that Monday morning.

He had befriended Ntombi before she was married to Simáo and he had not seen them for a long time. He had an open passport which allowed him to cross the border any time he needed to. GOD once again came through for me. It was no coincidence that Kobus and I met in that way. GOD'S plan and purpose was taking shape around me all the time.

That Sunday night I was introduced to the church council where I thanked them for their hospitality. Once all the thanking had taken place, they had a huge braai (barbecue) with meat like I had never seen before. I had a good sleep that night. The next morning after saying my goodbyes to Pastor and Mrs Manzini, Kobus came around and off we were to Ponto Mamoli, the province the mission station was in.

CHAPTER 7

GETTING ACROSS THE BORDER
MONDAY 2 AUGUST

From here on I will be writing a day by day report on how the LORD'S purpose for me going to Moçambique was fulfilled.

After my goodbyes I was left alone with one of the younger children waiting for Kobus van Schalkwyk. Time was ticking by and I was becoming anxious, so many thoughts went through my mind. Why would a man like Kobus offer to take me across the border, what went through his mind when he offered without even thinking about it. Why would he be so eager to get me across, we didn't know each other, we've never met before that afternoon. How did it come about that I met him, a Dutch Reformed Minister out there in Kwa Zulu Natal.

GOD had known that Simáo's bakkie would break down and that I would be stuck. GOD also knew that Kobus would be at that Anglican Church's dedication and that he had not seen Simáo and Ntombi in years. GOD had worked in Kobus's heart when I explained to him why I was there and where I came from, that he Kobus would offer to take me across to the other side.

GOD is good, HE is holy, HE is all knowing, HE is wonderful, fully involved in one's journey when HE sends you. HIS comprehension and understanding of the situation at hand no one can understand and HE tells us not to be anxious about anything. There's a song that goes like this "Who am I that you are mindful of me, how you love me, it's amazing". LORD I humble myself before YOU in awe of who YOU are.

It was 9.30am when Kobus arrived and after I had loaded my bags and said goodbye to the last member in the house, thanking her, we left and were on our way. Excited? Man what an understatement, I was ecstatic. We stopped at a supermarket in Manguzi on the way to the border. Pastor Manzini's house was about five kilometres before you got to Manguzi. Kobus and I became first name buddies in next to no time. We spoke both English and Afrikaans as we travelled. We bought a few items and six loaves of bread then left.

Further down the road we had to drive across a dam wall. The road takes a steep decline or incline depending on which direction you were travelling from and it was this road which ran across the top of the dam wall. What a beautiful sight to behold! The dam wall was built at the widest point in the river allowing access to the other side. Well it was not far from there that we saw the buildings of Cozy Bay border post jutting out above the terrain. Getting across the border was no problem as we both produced our passports and filled in the little destination slip allowing us access into Moçambique. Once again we were on our way, Whoopee!! We followed the dirt road which I remembered we took in June with the Suzi trip. This dirt road was fun, up and down, slowing down, speeding-up, through muddy water, around stagnant water which looked too deep and over the grass on the side of the track to avoid this treacherous looking water. There were sections of hard compact ground and a bit of tar here and there, and then the loose sand always at the top of an incline where you have to roll your vehicle through the sand. No high revving or the vehicle would get stuck in the sand.

I recognised Simáo's vegetable patch as we neared the homestead.Looking up the hill on the opposite side as we passed the vegetable patch, we saw the sign board "Igreja Communitaria de Moçambique". This is the name of the community orphanage run by Simáo and Ntombiyenkosi Mucache; We had to stop at the top of the incline as there was a log across the entrance on two "Y" shaped stumps blocking the entrance. I got out of Kobus's 4 X 4 to lift the log boom from across the entrance so that we could get through. As he drove through I expected him to wait for me as I dropped the boom in place again, instead he got so carried away by the moment that he drove right on into the drive-way next to the house.

I heard the hooting, the hellos and the laughter and as they were about to ask where I was, they saw me walking down into the drive-way. Once again there were jovial greetings, hugs and embracing. We were introduced to a missionary, Derek from Empangeni in Natal.

He had come all the way to tow the 4 x 4 bakkie back to Empangeni for repairs at the Toyota agents. As they left Kobus and Ntombi caught up with news from both sides and I unloaded my bags and then I joined them around a cup of coffee and biscuits. Kobus didn't stay too long because he wanted to catch up with the towing vehicle to assist them if they needed help. Ntombi showed me to a bungalow which ultimately became my bungalow.

I left my bags there and walked with her to the other side of the premises where I met Amelia and Rachel two Portuguese missionaries. They had been here for the past month of July and were to stay another two months till the end of September.

Before Simáo and Derek had left to go to Empangeni,Simáo and Ntombi had asked me exactly what I had in mind. Well I told them my main purpose was to build a playground for the children with a Jungle-Jim and hang four swings and thereafter tackle whatever else there was to do. Simáo said he saw my heart and appreciated me thinking about the children but he had a much bigger task for me. He asked me to follow him to the church building and we all then followed him. When we saw the building as we walked along the path he stopped and I was asked to look at the slope of the roof and he told me how the water streams like a torrent into the building.

He asked me to remove the roof and then to mark a new slope on the two sides along the width of the building wall. I would then have to cut the wood slats (a Wendy house type of walls) to the new angle and also to add two additional purlins (70 x 50mm wood supports) to reinforce the asbestos roof sheets. There were also two wooden poles 150mm in diameter that had to be straightened up as they were leaning outwards. The people who had built the original building had cut one of the rafters (220 x 50mm) too long and left it as it was, nailing it into position causing the outward bulge. The roof of course had to be put back on but re-spaced so that there was a bigger overlap at the centre joint. What a task!

I looked at Simáo and smiled, he knew he was asking something really big, taking everything into consideration. The reason why I was here and how I had arrived by bus was enough. No one had ever travelled to Moçambique by this mode of transport. He could see GOD`S purpose in sending them someone like me. Well guess whose smile was the biggest when I said ok, but I would do this task after the children's playground. Then I was completely taken by surprise by a loud emphatic "NO" first the church and then the playground. What could I say but "OK".

I realised that here was a man in authority to be respected and to be liked for his boldness. There was no space for "but I came here" or "why the church first" because as he explained this August month was one of the two months with not much rainfall. The sooner the church got fixed the better for them as there is no other building big enough to accommodate everyone on a Sunday morning.

Simáo introduced me to Makwakwa who was a local Preacher from the area and also one of the few adults on the premises, working and helping with whatever he could. I was told that I would get full assistance from Makwakwa and three of the bigger boys when they came from school. All these arrangements and discussions took us about 20 minutes. Before Simáo and Derek left with the bakkie he told me "if you have any problems speak to Ntombi".

After that I went to my bungalow and unpacked my bags and settled in as best I could. About an hour later I was called to lunch and sat together with Ntombi, Amelia and Rachel. The two Portuguese ladies were jovial and friendly. Rachel being younger than Amelia and speaking less English than her was at first a little shy. I soon made her see that I was in the same position as she was as I could not speak any Portuguese.

Food supplies were a bit on the low side because of Simáo's bakkie which had been standing for the past two weeks, he could not replenish supplies and we had to eat what was offered. I enjoyed lunch and then excused myself from the table and started getting the necessary tools together for my task.

Suddenly I stood still, why task, it does not sound right, as if I have to do it, and not as if doing it with a willing spirit. No! I will call it "my project". Now this is how it read in chronological order:

- Roof of church leaking badly.
- Incorrect roof slope.
- Too little overlap of asbestos sheeting at the centre joint.
- Roof sheeting to be removed.
- 2 x extra purlins to be added and same to be re-spaced to accommodate extra purlins.
- Wood slat walls to be cut at new angle.

- 2 x support poles to be set up straight, as they were sloping outwards.
- Roof to go back on with rectified overlap.

Yes "my project" sounds much better as it leans more towards my willing spirit.

That afternoon Makwakwa and I started removing the 4 roof screws on each sheet where we were later joined by the three boys whom Ntombi brought to me. I soon learned to remember their names, there was Fernando, short but very clever, quick to understand what was required. Dinho was a few years younger than Fernando but very willing. Then there was Domingos, the tallest of all the children also with a very willing heart, not talking much but very quick to understand. The three boys and I became very close friends.

We worked furiously that afternoon, removing all the roof sheets and packing them neatly on the ground in rows of 6 stacked on top of each other. We had logs underneath at each end so that they did not break lying on the uneven ground. Somehow we managed a day's work within half a day. We packed up and went to have supper.

We had supper together at the house, our adult group consisted of Amelia, Rachel, myself, Simáo and Ntombi, then there was also little Rocha who was Simáo and Ntombi's 2 year old son. I was to share supper with the group for the next month. What a pleasant thought, here at the table where we were seated I made a very interesting observation. It does not matter where your child grows up for here was a situation where things could so easily have been so much different, but with the grace of the LORD on this family it was good to be around that supper table.

GOD`S word says *"Teach a child in the way he should go and when he is older he will not depart from it".* All around here was bush and jungle area, while back home where I come from we have a concrete jungle all around. What I saw was that manners and etiquette does not come from the area you live in but from your parents' teaching especially your mother.

After a pleasant supper I was invited to join Ntombi, Amelia and Rachel in one of the bigger bungalows together with the children to have fellowship. Out here fellowship was prayer, worship and dancing, and then scripture reading and a short inspirational input by Simáo into the children's lives.I was also introduced to the children on that first night.

Although fellowship was always held in the church building, the venue had to be moved to the next biggest bungalow when the roof was removed. The electric current ran via a cable to a petrol operated generator. This cable had to be removed from the rafters causing the building now to be dark at night. Night time I found comes earlier than in Cape Town at that time of the year. By 18h00 it would be pitch dark outside, sunrise would be about 5.00am in the morning so that by 5.30am it would be so warm that you could not sleep anymore.

I watched and took note of how they worship and have fellowship out here. The younger children and the older girls would be sitting to the one side, but because there were so many, the group would sit right up to the middle of the room. The bigger and older boys would be standing at the back of the room, full of shy giggles and smiles. The Worship would be led by Mamma Katerina who was one of the senior women on the premises. The older girls would come around mamma and sing with her whilst the boys standing at the back would break into a dance. We could see that everyone was enjoying themselves, gone were the shy smiles as the dancers came into their own, dancing to the tempo of the songs to the point where you feel as if you are being carried away.

I would be sitting up front with Simáo in an honoured place, the other women, Ntombi, Amelia and Rachel with little Rocha sat with the children. Here in this room was another observation as the night carried on. Every now and then there was a slapping sound, I soon realised that while I would smear myself full of Tabbard, a mosquito repellent, they would slap this deadly insect before it could bite them. They had become so accurate and sensitive to these insects that slapping had become a natural part of their lives so that even the little ones were doing it. During the day one would never say that all these mosquitos were around.

Little Rocha would soon be getting tired and move over to his mother's lap and before long would be fast asleep. After the first session of dancing and worship Simáo would either talk to them or read out of the bible teaching them GOD`S Word. It was now nearly 21h00 and I was also becoming very tired, I said goodnight to everyone present and went to my bungalow. I tell you people, I was fast asleep before my head touched the pillow. I had a good solid night's sleep.

CHAPTER 8

GETTING TO KNOW MORE AND
LITTLE THINGS TO DO
TUESDAY 3 AUGUST

Today I had breakfast and fellowship with Ntombi, Amelia and Rachel. We had a pleasant and Blessed excitement of our sharing of our born again experience. Amelia and Rachel also spoke about how they had met Ntombi and countries they had been to. We said our thanks and Prayed for the safe return of Simáo from Empangeni.

Ntombi then asked me to check all their electrical tools and fix whatever was broken where I could. All the tools were kept in a shed which was kept locked. There were two jig-saws, and a skilled saw which were all working and an electrical plainer which was out of order. It was too complicated to fix without a tester, I used the portable generator for current.

Then I decided to repair and do alterations to the cupboard in my bungalow. When I had assessed what to do and how to fix the cupboard, lunch came up before I could start. There was so much to eat that after I had my fill, I had to say "no more thanks", far too much food. The saying goes that the way to a man's heart is through his stomach, but I am just not used to eating a big lunch at home during the week, a couple of sandwiches is okay with me, too much trouble fixing a lunchtime meal for myself. Please don't think I am ungrateful I just did not expect such a big meal.

Here it was just like in the early days when the Israelites had to eat up all the food on that day, for the next day it would not be good to eat. One could not have a refrigerator running as there was only current at night from 18h00 until 22h00 via the petrol generator.

After lunch I fetched Fernando to help me with the cupboard. When we were finished with the cupboard, altered, repaired, cleaned, fitted with new handles and a clip attached to keep the door closed, we brought it back to the bungalow. It was now in an excellent condition and looking good. As we were busy packing up Simáo came back from Empangeni in South Africa, everyone was glad to see him. We sat around talking and when supper was ready we ate and had fellowship together. We also thanked the LORD for his safe return from Empangeni in South Africa. Simáo had travelled all this distance on his motor bike.

Ntombi then told me to relax, make myself feel at home as if I was in my own home, also that I could make myself tea or coffee whenever I felt and generally have a free run of the whole property, fixing and repairing wherever I saw a need. After supper I went to bed early, sat a little with the WORD and then went to sleep.

CHAPTER 9

REALISING THE IMPORTANCE OF EARLY MORNING QUIET TIME
WEDNESDAY 4 AUGUST

This morning I got up early and did my morning thing like bathroom and getting dressed for the day's work. I had breakfast and saw Simáo already working on his Yamaha. I helped him for a while with a couple of screws but I did not feel good, the reason, I never had quiet time with my DADDY.

I collected all the tools I needed for the day's work from the tool shed and placed it in the church building ready for the day's work. Then, I left to fetch my bible from my bungalow and grabbed my cell phone and took a walk past the two bungalows where the children stayed. The younger boys with two of the older boys were in the one bungalow whilst the older boys were in the other.

As I carried on walking along the path through the shrubbery there was no fear of being mugged or confronted by someone wanting a cigarette or money from you. It was so peaceful and serene with a few chickens darting out of the way as I walked. There were a couple of odd pieces of rope with a tyre tied to it hanging from trees in that area. It was a good place to be in I thought, but not quite what I wanted. All of a sudden I walked into an open field; I was still following the path which stretched across to the trees and shrubbery on the bottom of the sloping ground about 150metres to the other side. There were places along this path where the grass was nearly as tall as me. I took all of this in as I walked looking at the different types of vegetation and trees compared to what you see back home. I am a very nature conscious person always enjoying GOD'S creation around me, even the concrete jungles we sometimes find ourselves in. Yes the cities with all its tall buildings where GOD had given man the wisdom and ability to build such huge clustered buildings, on top of one another and none of them toppling over.

Let's get back to where I was, yes, I get so carried away by the awesomeness of GOD'S Mighty hand in creating the earth. As I followed the path I started praying, praising, singing and thanking the LORD for His creativeness in thinking about the smallest and biggest plants suited to all the different areas. I walked further along the path, at some places overgrown with weeds and shrubbery. Here I had to stand still and look up ahead so that I could see the direction of the path. This path had obviously been walked on often when Simáo and the children had been building their bungalows and other structures.

As I walked up the hill on the opposite side and looked back towards the mission station on the lower hill, I realised it was more suited for where they had built the station than the one I was standing on now. I was by this time standing right on top of the hill and as I looked to my left, I saw the sea. What an awesome view all around me!

After basking in the beauty of the LORD, I tried to make contact with Theresa my wife; there was a good signal but no network. I felt disappointed but started singing, praising and blessing the LORD and thanked Him for Simáo and Ntombi's sacrifice out here in the bush or jungle or whatever you wanted to call the area. I left there and walked back to the mission station full of fire and ready for work.

In my bungalow in my bag was a dried guava roll Theresa had put in for me with a note for me to think of her whenever I felt for a piece of this roll. She called it "her sweet portion" Oh! How I love that woman of mine.

There were some Rooibos teabags and a biscuit to be had before I set off to carry on with "my project". As I entered the church building I realised that there must be so many people out there who never in their wildest dreams could imagine what it was like to get into GOD in such an awesome environment.

I began loosening some of the main wooden rafters. By this time Simáo had come over and we discussed the angle of the new slope. After debating and considering all aspects, including the new overlap for the asbestos sheeting, we came to a decision. There was a dilapidated step ladder which I used as best I could to make a mark. Simáo gave me a little spirit level which fitted neatly in his pocket with which one could draw a level line. I left to go to the tool shed and after looking and scratching around I found a 600mm long spirit level which I felt good about. I drew a level line with this 600mm level along the narrower side of the building which was actually the front of the building. The entrance door into the church was on the side we were busy on.

I knocked a 3" (inch) nail or 75mm nail as the measurement is used today in South Africa, at the other end of the line. I asked Simáo to judge what he thought was a good angle. The rope was tied to the nail knocked in the wall of the church. I then stretched the rope to the other end where Simáo showed me the exact position of where to knock the other nail in the other end. After Simáo had shown me where to knock in and tie the loose end of the rope for the new angle, I drew a pencil line using the spirit level along the rope. The rope was stretched as tightly as possible that the nails felt as if they would bend. This was to avoid sagging.

When the line had been marked and I was ready to start cutting with the hand saw, the children started coming home from school. They had lunch which was cooked by Mamma Katerina and one of the older girls staying on the premises. There was a sheltered area especially made where they had two fires burning with two huge pots on it. This was a daily routine which they would go through so that when the children came back home from school, the food would be ready for them.

I could not use the portable generator as it needed servicing, hence the handsaw and not the jig saw. Fernando helped me with the cutting. As we took turns, we worked until the light started fading, packed up and put the tools away. The hand cutting took a lot out of us, it was hard work and we were tired. I forgot to mention that before I started work that morning I took photos of the church building from different angles so that the building could be seen without the roof before I carried on further. The ladies were busy with the food so I snapped them as well as the women busy with the process of paper making not too far from where my bungalow was.

After we packed the tools away we washed our faces and arms and felt refreshed. Supper was to be another hour so I went to lie down a little while waiting. After supper we had fellowship and I later sat with Simáo and Ntombi and finally went to sleep, it was 9.30pm and because I was so very tired I was fast asleep before I knew it.

CHAPTER 10

USING THE JIG-SAW
THURSDAY 5 AUGUST

6.15am was a good time in the morning for the bathroom and to get going for the day. One gets used to the heat and can adjust oneself accordingly. Simáo and I had breakfast together. When breakfast was done I got all the required tools needed and took it to my project. Makwakwa also placed the "generate" as they called it at the church building. Simáo had serviced the generator the day before and it was running well.

Ntombi had suggested that I try using the jig-saw to see whether it might work better than the hand saw. After testing and checking it out we found that it worked well. I was quite fine with it as I had thought that the jig-saw would not work because of the way the wooden slats were assembled. From there we each went our separate way as we all had something or other to do.

Well it was now time for me to go and have quiet time with my DADDY. As I looked down the hill into the valley below, I saw this huge tree, not quite as big in height but big as in bulk. It was the kind of tree that one could see had been standing there forever, the main branches on this tree, were as thick as our trees back in Cape Town. Hanging from the tree were a couple of ropes with tyres tied to them, it seemed an ideal place to have quiet time.

My DADDY soon had me going into a deep spiritual time with HIM, how beautiful! I had placed a log that was lying there to the one side of the swings and pulled a few weeds out so that seating on the log would be more comfortable. I was not there too long, about half an hour and then went back to the house. It is not about how long one spends in quiet time but the quality of one's quiet time with the LORD that counts. At the house I had a mug of coffee with Simáo and Ntombi and then left to go work.

Ntombi's suggestion of the jig-saw worked so much better than the hand saw, it saved me so much time and made the physical work lighter. When the boys came back from school Fernando came over to help me. His help was very welcome, although it was difficult communicating however the language barrier was breached in the end. He was pleased because he was learning more English words as the day went by. I would ask him to pass me the hammer and he would stare at me with a blank expression, I would have to climb down from the ladder and go to where the hammer was lying, picking it up I would say "hammer" in English and he would repeat the word after me. It was not that he did not know what a hammer was it was just the language barrier. He saw there were nails to be pulled out at certain points as I moved along with the jig-saw, it was the language we had to master between the two of us and also the other two boys. At fading light we stopped and packed up and put the tools away. Simáo was busy fitting a few light bulbs around the buildings, I helped him and thereafter we had supper. After supper it was bed for me I realised that I had not taken my Malaria tablet, I quickly took it with water and went to bed.

CHAPTER 11

THE SPIDER AND THE WILD BOAR
FRIDAY 6 AUGUST

It was 6.15am and time to rise and shine again. After my bathroom stint I had breakfast, Ntombi told me again to relax and make myself at home and to take coffee or tea as I felt. I thanked her and went off to have quiet time with my DADDY. I prayed for my family at home and realised just how much I missed Theresa, we were very close, Jaime and Craig as well as Olivia were not far behind on the longing list.

Craig was born from my first marriage which ended in divorce after five years. Jaime was born to Theresa and myself after two years of marriage. There is a line of years in our dates of birth which was definitely not arranged by man. I was born in 1947, Craig was born in 1977 and Jaime was born in 1987. The number "7" is the heavenly complete number and all three our birth years ends with the number "7". The three of us are all walking with the LORD, saved, born again and baptised.

At the time of writing this book, I used to minister at a drug rehabilitation centre for youths, boys and girls as a motivational speaker and counsellor. Craig was the sound man (electronics) and also assisted the choir at the church where he worships. Jaime was a member of the dance and drama team which had also been going on mission trips. When he left school he joined this group of young enthusiastic youths called "Latreuo" headed by Pastor Suzy their leader.

The LORD has called the three men in our family for a specific reason. This reason I have come to realise has been designed by the LORD for us to be a blessing to those in need out there in various age groups and also where people need to be blessed by the HOLY SPIRIT.

Even my wife Theresa who is an actress, when she became born again, dedicated her talent to the LORD`S work and to be a blessing to many out there. She has been an inspiration to many a young person and even to the not so young.

I would like to add here that we have a daughter, Olivia who is the eldest of the three children. She is a senior nursing sister at a leading hospital in Cape Town. Bless her heart! She is dedicated in her vocation not just as a sister but also a blessing to the patients and staff with her loving and caring nature for those around her. HALLELUYAH!

After writing this portion about my family and I which was HOLY SPIRIT led, I asked JESUS to give me wisdom and strength for the day, I then prayed for everyone at the mission station and blessed them in the name of JESUS.

My time with the LORD had been such a revelation and blessing to me. I went back to the mission station which I was beginning to look upon as home. Simáo and Ntombi were busy having coffee and biscuits and I joined them. Just then Amelia and Rachel came back from the beach where they had quiet time with the LORD, I have yet to experience quiet time on the beach.

Well it was time to get all the tools together and begin working on my project. When I had cut quite a number of wood slats, I stopped to check the windows as I went along. As I was cutting further some of the windows came loose, and I realised that whoever assembled the structure just wedged the windows in position. I then had to go back to the tool shed to fetch some 3" (75mm) nails to secure the windows firmly in position in the roughly cut openings. After setting the first window in place, I started knocking the nails through the wooden frame and into the wooden supports around the window frames. I knocked the first nail and it bent, the second nail also bent, and by the time the third nail started bending I realised it was the window frame which was so hard. Again I had to go back to the shed to fetch the drill and a couple of drilling bits. After drilling two holes at the top and at the bottom, I could secure the frames with the same nails after straightening them. The wood used to manufacture the window frames was extremely hard, it was now obvious to me why the window frames were wedged in without nails or screws. When I reached the third window to drill nail holes, the generator stopped supplying current, it just would not run any more. While checking the generator to ascertain what the problem was, I discovered that it was fine but the plug was faulty. Simáo and I checked the electrical panel that the switch was attached to and found that all the wiring was in perfect order. I then carried on cutting the wooden slats by hand while Simáo went looking for a replacement plug, he could not find one because the plug had a special attachment to it, called a converter to enable the current to be re-directed from the petrol to the plug.

By the time I was ready to knock the rest of the window frames in position we were called to lunch. Simáo in the meantime had left to go to Manguzi across the border on his Yamaha motorbike. The reason was to get a supply of petrol and a couple of grocery items which were needed as well as a new plug for the generator at the hardware store. Out in the mission field one has to make something work when it breaks or find an alternative that could be used and at times do without if it cannot be fixed.Simáo has some jerry cans which he ties on to the bike, one on either side of the saddle and one on his chest. He had a big back pack on his back loaded with groceries. Because the 4 X 4 bakkie had gone in for repairs he had no choice but to use this mode of transport. He travelled twenty kilometres up and down on the South African side of the border on a tarred road. On the other side of the border stretched 25 kilometres of sand and muddy track on a heavily loaded motorbike 250CC. Yes here in Moçambique it is hard you have to have the tenacity and will power to go on. The word "easy" does not feature in their language. Nothing comes easy in the mission field!

As I am writing here I remembered the happenings in my bungalow that morning. It was about 4.00am that I got up to blow my nose in the dark. I went back to bed and got up later at 6.15am. It was light by this time and as I stepped onto the raffia/reed mat at my bedside I saw this enormous spider lying on its back with its legs wriggling in the air. I got such a fright that I nearly jumped onto the bed, I stood dead still looking at this huge spider and realised that it was in my eyes a giant tarantula. With fear setting in and the thought of "what do I do if the spider starts walking or running towards me", I gathered myself and bent down slowly to get my shoes from under the bed. Keeping an eye on the spider I with one movement put on my shoes all the while still watching the spider. I now felt a bit braver with shoes on my feet and moved slowly towards the spider. As I approached the spider I started lifting my right leg and stood carefully with my foot in the air over this monstrosity in my bungalow. I waited a little and watched and when it seemed to me as if the spider was tiring of wriggling its legs, my foot came down very hard and fast and my heel with careful aim crushed the poor thing. It went crunch and I felt its ugly mess under my heel. I now felt brave enough to fetch a stick outside and scrape it out and thoroughly destroy it. The ugly deed was done and I was not going to find out how harmless or harmful such a huge spider was, it was about the size of my open hand. Later when I told Simáo, he said I should just have got a stick and pushed it outside. It is here in the mission field that one realises what a city slicker feels like out in the mission field when confronted with something as big as that spider.

Every day so far I have had a different experience to the day before, but let's get back to lunch before I started my spider experience. As I entered to seat myself at the lunch table, Ntombi somehow looked very pleased with herself. I did not know what it was; it was not my place to question her.

That morning while we were busy at the church she took the Yamaha to do her Friday morning outreach at one of the villages about 5 kilometres from there. Everything went well and when she came back she had a big chunk of raw meat tied to her back. The villagers had seen a wild boar in their area and that morning decided to catch it. When Ntombi arrived there they had already slaughtered it. I did not know what kind of meat it was.

Well the rice was dished first then the gravy over the rice and then a few pieces of meat. To my surprise it was very delicious, succulent and simply "lêkker!" (nice) This was the first meat we had since my arrival there. With Simáo's bakkie not around he could not fetch the supplies that were needed. We had been eating either "stuiwe pap" (maize meal) with cabbage bredie (stew) or "stuiwe pap" with spinach bredie for the whole week. We had to eat or go hungry. Ntombi did her best, bless her heart! There were no other vegetables available as they were all too small and too young as they had only been planted recently. Yes! The mission field is not for the finicky, full of nonsense type of guy who is very choosy about what he or she eats.

After lunch I went back to my project and about 3.30pm Simáo came back home and told me he was going to Katwaan for the weekend. I carried on working until 5.00pm when I completed my day's work. When I arrived at the mission house, Simáo was all dressed and packed, ready to leave for Katwaan. He goes to Katwaan every weekend to be with the other group of people where he has also started a mission station.

Supper was ready by this time and after supper Amelia and Rachel went to the children to have fellowship with them. I stayed behind with Ntombi who decorated some of the paper cards they had been making on the premises. About 9.00pm we heard a commotion coming from the children's bungalows. We hurried down the path to the two bungalows which were about twenty metres from there. Ntombi discovered that one of the boys had hit a younger boy on his head with a stick while he was sleeping; his head now had a big bump on it and it was bleeding. The boy who had hit the younger boy had an older brother who stayed in the second bungalow with the other older boys. He was told what had happened and went from his bungalow to the other bungalow to give his brother a good hiding. Ntombi consoled the two boys and proceeded to treat the head wound and then prayed with them and sent them all to bed. I went to my bungalow which was about eight metres away and went to bed after the "drama in the jungle".

CHAPTER 12

THE TWO SETS OF VISITORS
SATURDAY 7 AUGUST

This morning I got up at 6.20am, did my bathroom thing and then had breakfast. After that I went to my spot under the tree to have quiet time with my DADDY. The LORD gave me a message for the Sunday morning service from the book of *MATTHEW chapter 18 from verses 1 to 7*. The scripture was about the children coming to the LORD and the mill stone tied around one's neck. I felt very positive and full of fire about the message and I was also ready for work.

The door handle on one of the children's bungalows was faulty. After an inspection I fitted a new handle and then went to work on my project. I had not been working long when some visitors arrived. Simáo's younger brother Joseph and a friend had arrived. We had lunch together and then they left immediately after lunch. I went back to work and about 4.00pm I had completed the side which was actually the long wall about ± 25 metres long. I had cut all the slats on this wall and felt it was quite an achievement. I packed up and went to my bungalow.

When I arrived there I found a sleeping bag, a rucksack, shoes and a bible in my bungalow. Ntombi, after I had enquired told me that there was a Pastor and three British youngsters who had arrived there about 3.00pm. She introduced me to the group. Their names were Johnny, Laura and Charlotte. I showed them around for they wanted to see how the people lived and survived out here. We sat around the two pots on the fire and fellowshipped around various topics.

We all had supper at the mission house, it was quite fun with Amelia and Rachel who were more in the dark about the visitors' accents. In the meantime there was another youngster who had arrived, his name was Domingos and he was at the bungalow when I came to sleep. After chatting to him he asked me to pray that GOD would make a way for him to get to South Africa to further his studies. While I was praying he stopped me and asked me to lay hands on his heart as there was something wrong with his heart, he told me he gets tired very quickly and that the HOLY SPIRIT, while I was praying, spoke to him and that was the reason why he asked me. Here was someone from another country, who did not know me from South Africa, but he trusted GOD and was obedient. We are blessed when we are obedient to the LORD. We all had a good night's sleep.

PRAISE THE LORD!

CHAPTER 13

THE MESSAGE
SUNDAY 8 AUGUST

I got up at 6.45am and did my early morning routine and then had breakfast. I then walked to my favourite spot to be with my DADDY, I also prepared myself spiritually for the message. As I walked back to my bungalow I met Ntombi and Amelia walking together and I asked whether I could have the service that morning as the LORD had already given me this message yesterday.

It just so happened that Amelia was to bring the message that morning but she was not fully prepared, also that she would prefer to hold the following Sunday's service. Ntombi agreed and I knew God had ordained that I hold the service that morning. The scripture for the morning was from the book of *MATTHEW chapter 18 from verses 1 to 7* as I mentioned before. I went to look for a nice size rock so that I could hang it around my neck. At 9.45am I went to Ntombi and together we walked up to the church building. We were fortunate that no rain fell throughout the week and this Sunday also the weather was just fine as I had not completed the cutting of the walls also the roof could not be replaced yet.

After all the children had been gathered, all neatly dressed in their Sunday best and we were all seated in the church we were able to start. Ntombi got the children singing and everyone present joined in and clapped hands she then opened with a prayer. Mamma Katerina was asked by Ntombi to lead the Worship and soon after the children came forward in groups to do various dances with the songs that they sang. As this was happening a number of adults and youths came from the neighbouring areas to join in with the others. Ntombi then read *PSALM 113* which was in line with the message of love, humbleness and kindness concerning all the children and our children. It was time for me to take the service. I stepped forward and Ntombi introduced me explaining why I was here.

I then took over and everyone was waiting to see what the rock was about. I called one of the boys to me and put him on my lap. Why I chose this little boy was because he always had a pleasant smile and we already started to take a liking to each other, his name was "Yuri". I also called one of the girls, Elisa to my side she wore a neat pale silky dress with a ribbon and a bow around her waist. I chose these two children to demonstrate GOD`S love for all children not just for little boys or little girls. JESUS told the disciples not to chase the children away but to bring them to HIM and HE blessed them as the KINGDOM OF GOD was made for little ones such as these.

The next two verses were for the adults and here I used the rock and hung it around my neck. As I read these verses I started moving down to the floor as if the rock was dragging me down into the depths. There were a couple of sniggles but Ntombi soon put a stop to it as she translated what I had just demonstrated. The following words were what made them sit up straight and realise that the LORD is serious about adults as well as children: *"Whosoever causes any one of these little ones to stumble or sin, that person might as well tie a millstone around his or her neck and jump in the sea and drown him or herself".*

I proceeded to explain what a millstone is and how it was used in the olden days to grind the wheat corn into flour. The message was very blessed and as I said earlier, GOD had already prepared the message. All praise, glory and honour belong to HIM. I then sang "JESUS loves the little children" and Ntombi joined in.

After this I made an alter call, anyone who had an ailment or felt sick should come forward. One mother with her three children came forward, the whole family was sick with running noses. I laid hands on this family and asked the LORD to come with HIS healing stripes and do a miracle in this family. The doctor was very far away and also very expensive for this poor and impoverished family. Her husband works away from home two days a week and comes home once a month.

It is not a nice thing to see the plight of the people out here, the mission field is not a holiday camp or for the soft hearted or the weak. One needs to have the compassion of the LORD to understand how people can still survive out here. I will write more about this subject in one of my later chapters.

There were some elderly women seated in the church and I found two grandmothers, one with a grandchild and asked them to come up to the front. I blessed them in the name of JESUS and thanked the LORD for sparing them all these years and to give them strength so as not to give up on their families. One could see the years of struggle and triumph etched on their faces, their skin almost like leather from being amongst the trees, bush and the harsh sun out here. No! It is not an easy life. There were also two men who came from a neighbouring area whom I also blessed and then handed the proceedings back to Ntombi who closed the service with a prayer and as custom asked the one who delivers the message to stand at the door and shake everyone's hand.

Outside the building all the women could gather and have fellowship while I spoke to the men and some of the youngsters who were there.

After the service I removed the nails holding the windows of my bungalow closed at night, I replaced it with two window brackets I found in the tool shed. By that time it was lunch time. After lunch I went to lie down for a short while. At 3.30pm Ntombi called and asked whether I would like to accompany them to the beach. We walked down a winding path through the brush and onto a dirt road which came down from the back of the hill I had been on in one of my earlier chapters. We must have been about an hour at the beach when Dinho came running to call us as some visitors had arrived. We had to hurry as best we could for we had about twenty children with us and also little two year old Rocha. When we got back we found that visitors from Johannesburg had arrived, they were three couples and their children travelling in a land rover and two 4X4 bakkies (vehicles).

They brought quite an assortment of goods with them there was some clothing, toys medicine and linen table cloths donated by a hotel which replaced their old cloths with new ones. This was a real blessing because we could now use these cloths to cover the stack of foam mattresses donated from a similar situation by a business in Durban. The visitors left not long after that as the light was starting to fade and they also wanted to be back across the border before it closed.

Supper that night was light snacks and coffee. We then went over to the children's bungalow and had fellowship with them and thanked the LORD for once again coming through for them and blessing them with people who cared and thought about those who were less fortunate. As we walked across to the mission house, the children ran and chased one another and as they went to sleep in their bungalows we heard Simáo's motor bike as it drove up the hill to the gate, he had just arrived back from Katwaan where he had spent the weekend. I sat around with everyone for a while and then went to sleep in my own bungalow. Simáo had been introduced to the English visitors earlier just before I went to sleep.

CHAPTER 14

THE TRUDGE TO MAPUTO
MONDAY 9 AUGUST

I got up at 6.15am and went to the stove to heat some water for coffee, with early morning breakfast for the British group. They were leaving that morning between 7.30am and 8.00am. About 7.15am Horatio, the group leader who was also the Pastor who brought them here came to say goodbye. We shook hands and hugged each other and wished each other well for the purpose that GOD called us, each in his own country. We all had breakfast together, nine of us and Rocha, Simáo's son. The visitors were not too happy to leave as they felt the time spent with us was too short to get to know us better. We finally said our goodbyes and saw them off along the path. Fernando, one of the boys, would come back later once he had directed them on the dirt road to Maputo, a long 300km away. We felt sorry for them but what could we do, there was no transport. Ntombi prayed a blessing on the group and that GOD would grant them favour on the road so that they would get a lift.

When they were gone I took a light splash in the bathroom and immediately went off to sit with my DADDY at my favourite spot. I had a blessed time proclaiming aloud over the valley that the goodness and blessings of the LORD would rest upon this whole area that the mission station is occupying. I ended off by asking my DADDY for strength and wisdom for the day ahead and then went to my bungalow. Later I went up to the mission house and had tea and biscuits with Simáo. We briefed each other about our day's work ahead, and I then left to collect my tools and was off to my project. As I was knocking in nails in the beams where I placed them I suddenly saw visitors approaching. They could not find anyone at the house and came over to where the sound of knocking attracted them.

The group had been passing through the area the previous day and had seen the children playing with a makeshift ball. They had stopped and offered their rugby ball to the children. With the children never having played rugby, this ball served well as a substitute soccer ball with everyone joining in. They were a family of six, father, mother, two sons and two daughters and a friend who had visited them that morning in Secunda, South Africa. There they had bought three soccer balls and a tennis ball, an exact replica as big as the soccer balls for the girls. I had never seen anything like it!

The group had come in two 4X4 bakkies and were just driving around and thought of the children and decided to buy the balls and deliver it themselves. How very thoughtful and unselfish, thinking and caring about others. GOD is good and HE never fails those HE loves. Ntombi said that there were always blessings coming their way. These balls were some more blessings they receive on a regular basis, always something different.

I opened the boom for them which allowed the two vehicles to come right in onto the driveway. Ntombi invited them in and showed them the paper that gets processed on the premises. There were also little gift baskets that she put together with various items in it including a few paper sheets rolled and tied with a strip of ribbon. She sold two of these and was very proud of herself, as the mother said that they have a friend who has a gift shop and promised more sales. After that we had tea before the visitors left. I immediately got Ntombi, Amelia and Rachel together and thanked GOD for sending people who cared and who sees the needs of others.

Well I went back to work and not long after that Simáo came back from Manguzi. Lunch was served about half an hour later and after lunch it was back to my project. I finished up late as I wanted to complete the section I had been working on. It was now 5:45pm and also time for the generator to be started up for the night's lighting. The generator gets switched off at 10:00pm every night, if you still needed light after that then you would have to light your lamp in your bungalow. We had supper and I was off early, to bed.

CHAPTER 15

THE GARDEN PATCH
TUESDAY 10 AUGUST

I got up at 6.20am and did my morning routine before having breakfast with Simáo. He told me that he was going to the vegetable garden a little later and invited me to come with him. As I was about to be off to have quiet time Simáo called me and I turned to follow him with my Bible in my hand. We walked talking, down the sand, dirt road, grass track, whatever you wanted to call it. We soon left this dusty dry track and began walking straight over the field to the vegetable garden. I was surprised to see just how big a piece of land was allocated for this purpose. It was situated right next to quite a big lake which filled up from the river flowing through the area. The garden was watered from this source.

Simáo had quite a variety of vegetables growing here, mostly young plants. There was spinach, lettuce, tomatoes, carrots, beetroot, cabbage, potatoes and onions. Then he had a fruit area immediately behind the vegetables, but not quite as big. This patch consisted of bananas, pineapples, avocado pears and paw-paws. The banana trees had big bunches of bananas on it but they were still too small to eat though. The avocado trees were the only other fruit trees that had started bearing fruit, these were also too young to eat. They were no bigger than the tip of one's thumb.

He then showed me around and I saw how the younger children under Mamma Katerina's supervision, watered the garden. They had huge watering cans which two of them needed to carry when it was filled with water. There was an old water pump standing there which had packed up some time back. I then wandered off into the garden to walk in between the beds. Each group of vegetables had its own rectangular layout which I called beds. I prayed "a blessing of multiplication" in produce so that they did not have to go for days without veggies.

After spending some time in the garden including the fruit area, I left Simáo and Mamma Katerina with the children to finish what they came here to do. The walk back was a bit strenuous as the path with its loose sand was mostly uphill.In this group of younger children was a boy who after asking Simáo about him, told me they had found him wandering around in the area and that he could not tell them who his parents were. There were a number of children who did not know who their parents were or where they had come from. These children now look to Simáo and Ntombi as their new found parents.

Simáo and Ntombi told me that they always first try to trace the parents but without success. The authorities in charge of that area had told them that it was because of children such as these that they were given permission to have the orphanage on the land allocated for it.

I went back to get on with my project. Well today lunch took a bit longer as Ntombi made us a lovely thick vegetable pizza. After lunch I went back to my project and later Simáo came around and helped us for a while and then left me and the boys to carry on till dark. I thanked the boys for their help and we prepared ourselves for supper.

We had spinach soup and spinach bredie (stew), deliciously made, fresh from the garden. I am not a lover of spinach but I must say I felt very satisfied when I got up from the table. We sat around and chatted for about an hour around coffee and I then went to bed.

CHAPTER 16

HOME CELL IN THE JUNGLE
WEDNESDAY 11 AUGUST

This morning I once again got up at 6.15am. I had slept well and realised that I have been awakening at about the same time every day. If you set your inner alarm knowing you have to depend on yourself, it seldom fails you. It is a mind set to set yourself a time and in your subconscious at a certain time whatever you have set to do, will happen. I had breakfast with Simáo and then left to have quiet time with my DADDY.

While I was in the presence of the LORD, the HOLY SPIRIT spoke to me about "home cell". This is what the HOLY SPIRIT laid on my heart; although it was good to be with the children all of the time, the adults needed to get together on their own and enjoy being in the presence of the LORD. After my encounter with the HOLY SPIRIT I first spoke to Simáo and then to Ntombi and when we came together I told them what the LORD had laid on my heart and immediately in obedience to the HOLY SPIRIT we agreed to have home cell that night. Simáo would be with the children for half an hour while we carried on, and then leave them with Mamma Katerina so that he could join us.

I got my tools together and left for my project. By the time I started working Simáo had left to go to Manguzi across the border to buy petrol for the generator, He had one can tied in a bag on his chest, one can on his back and two more cans, one on either side of his saddle. He also had another empty bag for some grocery items. I was amazed to see him on his Suzuki bike with a big smile on his face. Another action that he took in faith!

I realised what a sacrifice it must be for them to live out here. At the moment their vehicle was being repaired and somehow or other they still had to do the essential things they would have done with their bakkie. There was a factor that I realised they must have considered many a time. "Why must we battle like this, we can just pack up and head back to any of the towns and leave everything and everyone behind." They could make a good living back in the city. But no! They chose to go where the LORD sent them and not to ever disappoint those they had made a commitment to. GOD`S blessings and GOD`S willing spirit had come upon them and was there to stay!!! Hallelujah!

I carried on with my project where I had left off at the main doors. As I removed the wood slats above and around the doors Simáo came back with all the supplies he could carry. About a half hour later it was lunch again. I felt that I was eating too much but realised I needed the food as the workload was such that you needed to eat well. After lunch it was back to my project.

The three boys came over to help me when they came home from school. Simáo also came over to help with the door area but left to tend the garden when he saw us managing. At 5.30pm we packed up and called it a day! It was also time for the generator to be topped up with petrol for the night's electricity. The generator would run until 10.00pm and then be switched off as I mentioned earlier.

After supper Simáo had the WORD with the children and we prepared for home cell. Hallelujah! While we were waiting for Simáo visitors arrived. Instead of the visitors being able to join us for home cell, there arose a whole new situation and some anxious moments. There were two young men in their early twenties who arrived in a 4X4 bakkie. One of them Manuel, had grown up on Ntombi's parents' farm and had come out here to Ntombi knowing she had influence at the Embassy across from the border. His study visa had expired and by the time he had been able to reach there it would be too late. She had to write a letter confirming who he was and his purpose for being in South Africa. Simáo was not very impressed and told Ntombi that Manuel could wait till after home cell. As we sat there I could see Ntombi could not concentrate on what was happening around her. Here I decided to step in and told Simáo that it would be better if we carried on with home cell while Ntombi wrote the letter. He saw the sense of it and we then carried on while she left the room with Manuel.

By that time it was too late to do any praise and worship, I opened our meeting with a prayer asking GOD to bless the first ever meeting like this. I also prayed that this meeting would manifest and grow in the area. We already had the ice breaker with Manuel's entry into our meeting. This was not exactly what the ice breaker was meant to be but it had the desired effect because everyone was eager and excited to start talking. I asked everyone present to testify about a time in their lives when the LORD blessed them abundantly.

Amelia, Rachel and I spoke about how the LORD blessed us in our meeting up with Simáo and Ntombi and how we came to be there now. Ntombi had joined us by now as she had written the letter and given them some biscuits to eat while they travelled the night road through the bush. I told Simáo and Ntombi that they would be testifying at our next meeting, which would be the following Wednesday.

The WORD was from *MATTHEW 10 verses 1 to 20*. The message was about JESUS telling the disciples to go out and proclaim the message that *"The Kingdom of GOD is at hand and that they were to go just as they were, without extra money, without extra clothing and without extra sandals".* There is such a strong message in these verses for everyone who feels they have been called to the mission fields. Go in faith, trusting the LORD in everything and for everything in whichever area it is you find yourself. I trust the LORD that this message will be applied to every person who has the desire to go to the mission field.

I would like to make a valid comment about something or a new event that the LORD has instituted and blessed. It does not matter what subject or for what purpose this home cell meeting has come about, it is ironical that it always seems as if there is some force that tries to stop or disrupt what was meant for good and not for evil. We had not even started the meeting when along came an interruption such as the urgent letter. Things could so easily have gone the wrong way. GOD`S purpose for that Wednesday night could not be stopped because the evil one had been conquered 2000 years ago with JESUS' death and resurrection. There are different perspectives of what could possibly have gone wrong, but GOD`S purpose always prevails. Blessed be the name of the LORD!

I closed the cell meeting by praying GOD`S blessing on everyone present and thanking HIM for a fruitful evening. We had coffee after cell and felt full of joy the way the meeting turned out. It was the start we felt of many such meetings to follow. We said our good nights and were off to sleep. Prys die Here! (Praise the LORD!)

CHAPTER 17

REPAIRING THE JIG-SAW
THURSDAY 12 AUGUST

I arose at 6.30am and washed, had breakfast and then quiet time where I asked my DADDY for wisdom and strength for the day's work. Simáo had packed early to go to Manguzi to buy petrol for the generator and a few items for the house. Ntombi called me aside to talk about last night's episode with Manuel it was a very interesting discussion of how he came to live on her parents' farm.

I got my tools together and started working on my project. The day before we had tied a nylon rope stretched tautly across the length of the wall. I took a pencil and marked a definite line for cutting so that the rope could be removed. When the boys arrived we carried on assembling the area around the doors. It was quite an effort and I could see the boys were very satisfied with themselves.

Simáo had at some stage serviced and reset the big generator because it was using too much petrol, about 10 litres in four hours. I started cutting using the jig saw, I had to go slowly so that the blade could be used without forcing it. Every second slat of wood was recessed so that the jig-saw blade just managed to reach it. The skilled saw blade could not reach there it was still a lot quicker and easier than with the hand-saw. After cutting a while I noticed that the jig-saw blade was going all over the place and I was not able to cut further. I had a look to see what the problem was and noticed that the little guide wheel that the blade runs on was missing. There was a little pin like an axle that the missing guide wheel runs on, this wheel was fitted in such a way that when the jig-saw is switched on the blade would run up and down on this wheel.

I was so relieved and glad when I eventually found the wheel lying on the floor on the inside of the building. Well, as I said before, in the mission field we fix and repair or salvage whatever breaks down, if there is a way to do it. Back to the tool shed I went with one of the boys, there we found another jig-saw with the same problem. After scratching around in all the boxes and finding nothing to substitute for the little pin, a brilliant idea came to me. Looking at all the nails in the various packets I found that the 3" (75mm) nail I tried was the exact thickness where there was no play on the little wheel and that it fitted snugly in the two holes in the holding bracket. I used the flat head of the nail as a stopper on the one side and asked Fernando to hold the jig-saw for me as I attempted to cut the nail. With Fernando holding the jig-saw placed on the vice, I used the cutting edge of the pliers and a hammer and knocked the pliers until the nail was cut to the correct size. We turned the jig-saw on its side with the head of the nail flat against the vice and used the hammer to knock the cut edge. I felt very satisfied because the new pin could not come out from either hole on the bracket. Fernando showed me the "thumbs up" sign with a big broad smile!

Back at the church building we plugged the jig-saw into the "generate", as I explained earlier, it was the boys' pronunciation of the word generator. I switched the jig-saw on and tested it on a piece of wood lying on the ground and voila! It was in perfect working order. We were back in business!

When Fernando told Domingos and Dinho what I had done, I could see a new respect in their eyes, realising how I had benefitted the mission station in these past twelve days. There were two more jig-saws in the shed with the same problem, the difference was that the little guide wheels were missing. It was another hour when the light started fading, we packed up and went our separate ways, the boys to switch on the generator and I to my bungalow. Supper was called and I told Ntombi that I was tired of the day's work and thanked her and the Portuguese ladies. It was straight to bed for a deserved night's rest.

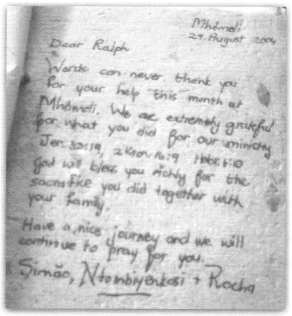

Letter of Thanks From Simáo and Ntombi

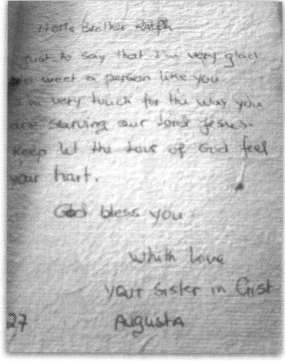

Letter of Thanks From Augusta

Drawing by One of the Boys at the Orphanage

Simáo, Ntombi and Guests

Local Women who worked on the Paper Project

Church Ceiling Repaired

CHAPTER 18

THE DAY I WOKE UP WITH A SPLITTING HEADACHE
FRIDAY 13 AUGUST

I woke up with a mind blowing headache; my head was throbbing as if being knocked with a hammer. It was 6.20am and when trying to focus I realised that I had not taken my Malaria tablet the night before. I had been so tired that I forgot about the tablet. I went to the kitchen and took the Malaria pill and two Panado tablets. After going to the bathroom I really did not feel up to anything, I was feeling nauseous and went to lie down as I did not want to vomit as I had taken the Malaria pill. About 8am I woke up feeling a bit better and decided to get some breakfast to help the pill to work through my system.

I went back to my bungalow and had quiet time with my DADDY I asked the LORD for strength and a clear mind for the day's work. Then I got the tools together and went to my project. After setting myself up I started the "generate" and proceeded to cut the slats on the entrance side. The cutting was going fine until I came across slat after slat with excessive gum inside the wood. The problem was that the blade would clog up with gum and after every slat I had to clean the blade before carrying on. I did not need this hassle as I was not feeling well yet. I carried on cutting until lunch was called.

I certainly was not feeling well yet and had a small lunch and took two more Panado tablets and went to lie down. I fell asleep and slept for just over an hour. On waking up I went to see how far Fernando got with the three poles I asked him to cut shorter. He had finished cutting it and was waiting for further instructions. I marked the buff joints on the uprights and showed him what to do. We took turns cutting the joints as we had to use the hand-saw and a chisel for these joints. The three boys then helped lift the rafters in position on top of the poles. I then knocked in 4 inch (100mm) nails to secure the rafters to the poles. By this time it was time to pack up. The boys took the tools to the tool shed while I marked the new spaces for the five purlins so that by tomorrow I would just have to nail it in position.

Fernando and the boys switched on the generator for the night lighting and I went to freshen up, tired of this stressful day. Supper came up and I went back to my bungalow for an early night praising and thanking the LORD for bringing me through the day.

CHAPTER 19

FEELING GOOD AND ON TOP OF THE WORLD AGAIN
SATURDAY 14 AUGUST

I got up at 6.40am and felt good! Yesterday was gone and behind me, I carried on with my morning bathroom routine and then had breakfast. I then proceeded to wash my washing which was long overdue. I strung a rope washing line from a tree behind my bungalow to the corner of the bungalow and used this as my wash line for the rest of my stay.

Then I asked Ntombi who would be holding the Sunday service. Amelia who was supposed to preach last Sunday would be preaching. But if she could not make it would I be willing to hold the service. I left to go down to my favourite spot under the tree singing and as I walked the HOLY SPIRIT spoke to me.

Peter and John had been fishing all night and did not catch anything. As they came in to shore they met JESUS who told them to go out again and cast their net on the other side of the boat. They said they had been out all night yet went back into the sea because of obedience to JESUS. Their catch of fish was so huge that they had to call for help as the net was too heavy for two men to haul in. The message that came with this scripture *Be obedient to the instruction given by JESUS and you will always be successful.* This scripture comes from the book of *MATTHEW chapter 4 from verses 18 to 20.*

There was a second message from *JOHN 21 verses 1 to 8.* If JESUS comes your way and asks you to follow HIM as HE asked Peter and Andrew and tells you HE will make you fishers of men, would you leave everything behind and go to follow HIM or would you first go and make arrangements to see that everything was ok and only then follow HIM?

However Amelia said that she had already prepared a message. Everything was well as I realised that I had a good message for home cell on Wednesday. Praise the LORD! Ntombi then told me they were off to the beach with the children.

I managed to fit one purlin and about 2½metres of the next purlin when lunch was called. We had lovely mince bredie(stew) the Friday night and now had the rest of it with a nice salad. Ntombi told me that Simáo had brought the mince and some meat with him and that the meat had to be eaten as quickly as possible because there was no refrigerator. A refrigerator could not function properly, there being current only at night for four hours. This is one of the hassles of being in the mission field. It was also Augusta's birthday that day and she baked a lovely cake. Out here cake is really appreciated.

There were also four seats for the swings Ntombi wanted for the children but only enough chain for two swings. I fitted the two swings on two of the branches of the huge tree under which I have my quiet time. As I wrote in one of my earlier chapters this tree's branches were as thick as some of the trees back home in South Africa.

This was the first opportunity I had of actually doing what I came out here to do, hang the swings and build a big Jungle-Jim for the children to play on. As I was still adjusting the seats, stepping back to see whether the seats looked level, two of the little girls jumped on the swing. The seat sagged sharply on the one side as the nuts on the bolts holding the chain to the seat bracket had not been tightened yet. They fell to the ground with a very surprised look on their faces but laughing as they got up. I of course had to reset the seat again before tightening it. This time they waited until I showed them the "thumbs up" that it was ok to swing on them.

There was a light supper prepared although they blessed me with the last plate of mince food. We sat a little around the table with a cup of coffee just enjoying each other's company. We then said our good nights and left for our bungalows.

CHAPTER 20

RELAXING AT THE BEACH AFTER CHURCH
SUNDAY 15 AUGUST

I got up at 6.40am and again felt good! The morning routine went quickly enough and I then went to breakfast. Ntombi joined me and told me she was worried about no lock-nuts on the bolts of the swings. After breakfast I scratched around in the tool-shed and found nine nuts which were enough for the eight bolts on the swings. She felt much happier! Once that was done I got my week's clothing together to be washed after service and then went to have quiet time with my DADDY.

The HOLY SPIRIT gave me a WORD from *ISAIAH 25 verses 1 to 5*. After thanking the LORD I got ready for church, I was pleasantly surprised when I arrived there. The children had neatly packed the chairs out and swept the floor picking up all the saw dust and sand from the continual work I was doing on the building.

Amelia had prepared a good sermon on "OVERCOMING YOUR FEAR". Her scripture reading was from *ISAIAH 4 verses 8 to 10*. She testified about her own fear at the airport in Portugal before coming to Moçambique. The plane they were sitting in waiting for take-off had some fault and the pilot was not sure whether they would make it. The passengers were told to either disembark from the plane and buy another ticket and take the next flight or they could remain on the plane and take their chances. The airways would not be responsible should anything happen.

The pilot told the passengers that the plane would be flying as scheduled and that should there only be one passenger, they would still fly. The passengers all sat and discussed the situation, then, one by one they began to leave the plane. There were only half the amount of passengers left and Amelia and Rachel were two of them. There were lots of prayers said, mostly about putting the plane and the pilot in GOD`S hands and that everyone would land safely. They had to put their fears aside and trust and have faith in the LORD. Well it is obvious that the plane arrived safely as she would not have been able to tell this story. Praise be to GOD! After Amelia's sermon Ntombi read *PSALM 66 verses 1 to 4* and I realised that *ISAIAH 25 verses 1 to 5* was confirmation of *PSALM 66*. Praise the LORD! We ended the service with two songs led by Mamma Katerina and Ntombi closed with a prayer.

After church I did my week's washing and as I finished, lunch was called. We had a good lunch discussing the service and how we were all blessed by it. When we were done with lunch, Ntombi and I had a very interesting discussion about relationships across the colour line.

She had grown up with black people living and working on her father's farm. She grew up playing with them and speaking their language and doing just about everything with them. So a marriage across the colour line was not too "far-fetched" or surprising when Simáo proposed to her. I won't go into detail here as they are happily married with a son, Rocha. They understood each other fully as they had both been called by GOD to this project they were busy with.

I had grown up a normal little "coloured" boy as we were called back in those days. There were quite a number of conflicting stories told about the "other people" which you as a small child accepted as you grew up with these different people around you. Only when I was a teenager and ready for work did I realise that we are all human beings, no matter how we looked. It did not really matter to me when I was still in primary school as there were children living in the same street diagonally across from us with whom I used to play. They were dark skinned partly African and I had a much lighter complexion than them. Their parents were inter-racially married as every colour and creed were labeled and classified by the old system. To me they were children across the street with whom I had a fairly good relationship. I did not realise it then, but now that I am writing this journal I realise how long ago I had accepted people of another colour into my life.

When I was in my early twenties I went to work at a nationally situated neon sign company. They had six adult Xhosa speaking men working at their branch in Cape Town. When I joined this company they were renowned for their glass tubing letters. I did not know anything about this neon section of the company. I was taught by two of the senior glass blowers and by this one guy named Clifford. Clifford and I were to become close working compatriots. He had been working in the glass blowing department for nearly 25 years. Although he was not a glass blower he knew everything there was to know about glass blowing and how to draw it. He was a good teacher and he really liked me as he saw that I was willing to be taught by this "black" man whom I should have looked down upon as stupid.

That was how some people saw other people of colour, me, I saw here was a man, a human being who knew his job through and through. He was very thorough and understanding, this was my first experience of the other side of the "black man" as they were known. I had no qualms about having to ask him when I was stuck. This was a period of time that the country was in uprising against the oppressor. He was passing on all his knowledge to me, a person of colour. I came here to this neon company without any knowledge or experience working with a black man. The understanding, knowledge and intellect of this black man, was way beyond me.

From this period on in my life it was all systems go as far as working, eating, laughing, joking and just getting to know Clifford and the other 5 guys working at this sign company. This time in my life was a time of training and accepting others as GOD accepts everyone, although I was not "born again" for many years to come.

To get back to Moçambique, this is one of the reasons why I could accept and fall in love with Simáo, Ntombiyenkosi, the children and adults at "Igreja Communitaria de Moçambique" the Mission Station. Looking back to what I wrote in the previous paragraph I realised just how long ago GOD had his hand on my life. What I do know is that GOD has plans for our lives, HE ordains our footsteps while walking, guiding, teaching, showing us just how deep the depth of HIS love is for us. I was destined then already! HE writes the days of our lives even before we are born, also HE walks with us through all situations we find ourselves in so that HIS purpose in our lives can be fulfilled for HIS glory. Hallelujah!!!

I will carry on now where I stopped after the interesting conversation with Ntombi. I told her that I was going down to the beach and was prepared to take the children with me. Two of the boys stayed behind, one was too small and the other had a disposition and because of this he was rejected by his parents and was brought to Simáo and Ntombi. One of the three dogs on the premises followed us to the beach, he ran up and down between the children and I. This male dog and I got to be quite friendly with each other, he always followed me around when I went for walks, running up to me and I would have to stroke his head and talk to him before he would leave me. Ntombi was very grateful to me for taking the children with me as it would give her a well-earned rest with Rocha.

It was quite a winding path through the stretch of high grass until it ran into an overgrown dirt road with two tyre tracks running parallel to each other and a grass verge running between them. We passed a project that was started as a tourist resort with a few bungalows standing in a group close to each other. There was also one bigger bungalow which one could see into through the open windows. This bungalow consisted of two bedrooms, one office, a bigger size kitchen than normal, a reception area and a neat stoep (porch) with a veranda. Apparently the whole project was stopped by the authorities and everyone involved was told to leave. They felt that the people concerned would be making a fortune. It does not matter where you go in Moçambique, somewhere along the line there would be drama.

As we passed this site there was a sudden decline, which was very steep with plenty of loose dry sand. At the bottom of the decline lay the beach, the dirt road or track as it can be called carried on past this steep slope to disappear over the top of another steep hill. There was no wind on the beach, how beautiful it looked! A long stretch of open beach to the right and the left of me with waves rolling in gently in the shallow water. I stripped to my boxer shorts and ran into the water with the younger boys following. The water felt so good that if someone had been watching they would not have known who was adult and who were children. Man! Two weeks of hot, humid weather and wow! As we say here in South Africa "lêkkerrr waterrr!"

Some of the older boys played soccer in the sand with one of the soccer balls they brought along. After a while of body surfing with almost every wave as it washed up on the beach, "lêkkerrr" I played a little with the boys in the water and after a while decided to leave the water to play some soccer with the other boys. I called all the younger boys out of the water as I was not really a swimmer, but liked to play around in the waves not too far from the shore, as sea water can be treacherous.

I never knew how unfit I was until a started playing soccer in that loose sand, eventually I was falling down more from exhaustion than tripping in the sand. We were laughing more than the entire time I had been there with them. I even tried to grab hold of them as they ran past me. Shoo! I hadn't enjoyed myself so much in a long time.

I went back into the water to rinse the sand off my body, dried myself and decided to walk towards the younger boys who had walked further down the beach. There were quite a number of strange looking shells lying around. I found an old plastic bag amongst the debris which one could see had been washed up on to the beach. As I started collecting the shells Dinho came up to me walking and kicking the ball. He helped me willingly to collect shells, some odd bits of dried out sea plants and pebbles. We met up with the boys and I called them as I turned back towards the path back home. It was a very pleasant and enjoyable afternoon.

When we arrived back at the mission station I cleaned up and hung out my wet towel and clothes. Ntombi was working in the dining room when I entered and I said that she should not worry about supper as I will just make myself some peanut butter sandwiches and coffee. Ntombi was pleased and asked the girls whether sandwiches would be "ok" and their answer was "yes". Ntombi made some salad and offered us frikkadels (meat balls) she had made.

After supper Amelia and Rachel went to pray with the children, Ntombi later joined them while I went to my bungalow. I started filling in my journal and while sitting on my bed I saw a movement on the wall between the slats. It was a rat-like face that was looking at me I got a fright and jumped up calling Domingos. We both looked and after scratching all over, could not find the rat. Domingos went back to his bungalow and I carried on with my journal not concentrating as before but nervously writing and glancing all around not feeling as secure as before.

Yes everyday there is some kind of drama or something that a city guy is not used to. As I said before the mission field is not for the weak or finicky! Simáo arrived at 9,40pm from Katwaan where he spent the weekend at the other mission station he had started. I greeted him and went to sleep.

CHAPTER 21

THE START OF THE NEW WEEK
MONDAY 16 AUGUST

This morning I got up at 6.20am in good health and feeling better as there was no disturbance from the rat I saw. At the bathrooms I met Mamma Katerina who told me that there was no water from the taps and that I should use the water in the green water tank standing on stilts behind the house. I did a quick splash as this water was so cold as if it came out of a refrigerator. This coldness was caused by the cold night air when the temperature drops quite low.

I had weet-bix and two slices of peanut butter bread with an apple as there was no water for coffee. I left to have quiet time with my dear DADDY and thoroughly enjoyed it as I read *PSALM 106, all 48 verses*. Out here your time is not as rushed as in Cape Town, you can go all the way with the LORD instead of a few minutes here or an hour there as one would sometimes do in Cape Town to squeeze in quiet time. The LORD spoke to me through this psalm revealing a lot to me, a real blessed time. Praise the LORD! I then got my tools together and went to work on my project.

I still had three purlins to mount on the rafters and a few joints to be reinforced. Simáo came to see what I was doing and while we were looking for extra pieces of purlins, visitors pulled up with their vehicle. They were from Alberton, South Africa. Simáo had helped a couple with directions the day before and as they passed by they saw the signboard from the road. The couple came back and decided to look at the children's home to see whether they could help out. Simáo introduced the couple to me as I started leaving to switch off the "generate" The reason there was no water that morning was that for three consecutive nights the boys had not switched on the water-pump and as a result, the big water tank ran empty. There are two switches against the wall in the generator room the one operates the generator and the other the water-pump.

I went back to my work and saw the visitors leaving a little while later. Simáo came over to help me and told me that they had offered to take him to Empangeni the next morning to fetch his bakkie as the man had business to attend to there. Ntombi and Simáo were so happy that they thanked the LORD because he would have gone on his motorbike, but now Ntombi and Rocha could go with.

We do not know how things work out so well, but there is one thing for certain; *ALL THINGS WORK OUT FOR THE GOOD* when you worship the LORD GOD Almighty. Praise the LORD! Simáo left after two hours of work to check on his garden patch. When he came back I whistled and called him over. I had one asbestos sheet on the roof and was not happy with the way it fitted. We measured the length of the sheets and the width of the roof and discovered that the third purlin had to be moved about 50mm further up to allow more overlap on the two sheets. We did not check the roof sheets when I fitted the extra two purlins. I stopped working and packed up as the light was now fading fast.

Supper was called and oh! How delicious, beans soup and beans bredie(stew) with salad. Man, I must say we were eating like kings and queens out here and it was all due to Ntombi's cooking that we felt this way. After supper Simáo, Amelia and Rachel went to pray with the children. Ntombi and I discussed the Jungle-Jim I wanted to build when I complete the church building. She made a rough sketch of how she would like it to be, suited for the little ones as well as the older and bigger ones. Out here there is always thought for all ages in everything, although there are times when we have to consider the adults on a long term basis which benefits all. We chatted a while longer and had tea and biscuits as the hour of 9pm had arrived. I said good night and left for my bungalow.

"GOD Bless You!"

CHAPTER 22

THE BAT AND I
TUESDAY 17 AUGUST

This morning I got up at 6:25am and again felt good. Simáo, Ntombi and Rocha would be getting a lift to the border. Praise be to the LORD! Simáo had helped a man on the road who had been stuck for some reason or other. He had checked to see why the truck they were travelling in had come undone, found the problem and fixed it. The man could travel on from there. This man had wanted to know where Simáo had come from and where he was going. When Simáo told him about his predicament of getting to the border and from there getting a lift to fetch his bakkie, this passer-by offered to fetch them in the morning and take them to the border. Clearly GOD had come through for them again!

Kobus my friend who had brought me across the border had made arrangements to meet them there and take them that morning to Empangeni. Everything went off well and at 7:30am they drove out through the gate.

I went back to my bungalow to have quiet time. I felt in my spirit that my time with the LORD was nearing its high point. Suddenly I saw a movement out of the corner of my eye, there looking at me was a nose and two eyes between the slats where the roof and the corner pole meet. I got up and slowly walked across to the stick on the cupboard. As I approached, the creature retreated up behind the rafter. I took the stick and stabbed it a few times up into the gap between the slats. The stick broke and as I turned to look for another stick, I heard a dull thud coming from the corner. I stopped what now? I slowly stepped across, almost on my toes, all nervous not knowing what to expect. There was a mattress lying in the corner and I could not see anything and as I was moving the mattress away from the corner I was expecting a rat to run out. Me, I was all nervous with the broken stick in one hand, what I saw lying on the floor stunned me. As I nervously peered down at the creature I saw that it was dead with its guts hanging out, I had apparently pierced its stomach with the jabbing of the stick. There on the floor was a bat! Its ugliness lying there exposed in such a gross way, "sies". It had been living in my bungalow for the past four days. Shoo! What next? I was so relieved that I had seen that movement because I had been very uneasy the past four nights in my bed. After disposing of the ugly creature, I washed my hands and closed my quiet time with a thank you prayer. What a ha! ha! event this was, once more a city slicker not knowing much about bats.

Well after that it was back to getting my tools together and off to my project. The second purlin was not a problem to loosen and then move it 50mm closer to the bottom edge as Simáo and I discussed yesterday. With that completed I went to sort out the poles I needed for the Jungle-Jim and found quite a number of them, although I felt that they were not enough as the more poles I had, the bigger I could make the Jungle-Jim. Ntombi told me I should ask some of the younger boys to help me carry the poles to where I would be working. There were eight boys with me, but when they realised why I called them, like all children, one by one they disappeared. There were so many places they could go that I did not feel like looking for them and now there were only two boys left to help me.

We carried the poles about 100 metres to an area next to the church where I was working on the roof. The boys and I went looking all over for poles. I would never have found so many of these poles which were lying around, without the help of the boys. After we carried them all up to the church, I rewarded the two boys with a sweet each. The other children looked very sad they knew they had lost out because they did not want to help.

I went to fetch the machetes to cut the bark and little pieces of twigs from some of the poles. I also brought the drill and a couple of drilling bits to drill the socket holes on the uprights for the ladder. The poles were long enough for me to cut 10 rungs spaced at 300mm between the rungs. This ladder was at a later stage to become the main support of the Jungle-Jim. When I was ready I started up the "generate" and did as much of the drilling as I could. It was already late afternoon when Fernando arrived. It was not long after that I packed up, with Fernando's help, to put the tools away. By this time it was nearly supper time. I tidied myself and carried on writing in my journal until supper was called.

We had the beans soup and food that was left over from the previous day, we did not complain but I must say the beans were beginning to feel heavy. In the mission field if you have to eat beans for a week, you cannot complain. After supper I retired to my room with a cup of coffee to complete my journal. I soon felt tired and went to sleep.

CHAPTER 23

THE HOLY SPIRIT AND THE RAIN
WEDNESDAY 18 AUGUST

I arose to a wet, cool morning it had rained during the night. When I was done with my morning routine and had breakfast, it started to rain again. The place for my quiet time was decided for me by the rain. It was to be in my bungalow, I not knowing what was to follow later this rainy morning.

With a cup of coffee and a slice of peanut butter and jam bread I was off to my bungalow as fast as I could move without spilling too much coffee. I then had a very nice time with my DADDY while the rain came down harder and harder. The decision I took not to work on this rainy day was the correct one, I decided to take the cup and plate back to the kitchen. As I stepped in by the door the rain now really started to fall hard, I sprinted back to my bungalow under an ever increasing amount of water falling, being careful not to fall. After drying myself I decided to spend some time with the WORD.

The HOLY SPIRIT directed me to *ISAIAH 55 verses 10 and 11*. I opened the bible to write down the information in the front of it. "The Topical Chain Study Bible, New American Standard by Thomas Nelson Publishers". This is the bible that Pastor Henry Manzini loaned to me unselfishly when I left his house for Ponto Mamoli. Why I used the word "unselfishly" was because this was his personal bible. He said it was fine as he had some more bibles in his study. What an honour and pleasure for me to have this very informative bible for a whole month.

I must have a special mention of these two verses in that the rain falling this morning it was the perfect analogy. GOD speaks to those who are thirsty for HIS WORD. The verses:

"As the rain and the snow come down from heaven, and do not return to it without watering the earth and making it bud and flourish, so that it yield's seed for the sower and bread for the eater, so is my word that goes out from my mouth: It will not return to me empty, but will accomplish what I desire and achieve the purpose for which I sent it".

My DADDY is faithful and true, always ministering to us through HIS HOLY SPIRIT as HE pleases and the wonder of our FATHER is that HIS moment is always perfect. Hallelujah!

Yes I spent some time in deep ministry with the LORD. As the rain came pouring down the wonder of it all was that I sat wearing only a sweater and a shirt, there was no need of a jersey. This was their winter and they called it cold. I got very involved with my DADDY as I sat on the bed, a new revelation was revealed to me whilst reading the whole chapter of *ISAIAH 55 verses 1 to 13*. I was taken away so far that I started crying loudly in my room and singing to my LORD from joy and happiness and the LORD`S mercy and grace. I thanked the LORD and then there was a break in the rain.

Being so long in my room this morning I had noticed cracks and openings in the building's walls and decided to get a hammer and nails so that I could nail down loose boards and close up all the cracks. There was quite a bit of draught in the room coming from all sides. I would have to see whether the nails and hammer had done the trick. It must have been about ten minutes after I had finished this operation when it started raining again. I decided to climb into my sleeping bag and doze off. I fell fast asleep and woke up about 12:15pm with it still raining.

Lunch was called at 1:00pm. It was both Rachel and Ntombi's birthdays today. After wishing Rachel we had lunch, delicious bean soup and salad, whilst enjoying lunch it began to rain so hard as if someone was standing with a bucket and pouring the water out of it. This morning's heavy shower was nothing compared to the amount of water falling outside now. We finished lunch and had to wait for the rain to subside.

I decided to put up a shelf in my room as the rain had by this time stopped so that I could collect some off-cuts from the slats of the church and two lengths of 38x38mm battens. As I was about to start Simáo, Ntombi and Rocha stopped outside in the 4x4 fully loaded with various items needed for the house.The bakkie had been repaired by a Toyota dealer in Empangeni.

They brought the roof nails and also more chains for the children's swings. After chatting for a while, Simáo decided to work on his Yamaha. I came back to my bungalow to build the shelf, it was now past 5:00pm with the sky completely clear only the wetness of the ground was evidence that it had rained.

At the supper table we decided to erect the roof in the morning. Hallelujah! The mosquitoes had been buzzing around me from all angles earlier and I had to fetch a mosquito coil for the night. Supper was so delicious it felt like a Sunday meal at home in Cape Town with rice, sausage and beef bredie (stew) also fruit salad from the garden, paw-paw, bananas and apples.

We went over to the children and partied with cake, tea and coffee, after that we all said good night and went to our own rooms and houses for a good night's rest.

CHAPTER 24

THE CHILDREN AND THE ROOF
THURSDAY 19 AUGUST

I arose this morning at 6:30am and did not feel too good. My stomach was not feeling well, a bit of diarrhoea which made me run to the toilet. I drank some medicine (Jamaica Ginger) which helped to stabilize the cramps I was feeling. I then decided to get down to my regular routine and get on with my life! Why I mentioned the word "diarrhoea" which might not sound too nice, out here we have to name the ailment so that others out there can see what we as missionaries have to go through. There is actually no time to be sick when you are out in the mission field. You take whatever medication if it is necessary and move on instead of going to lie down and be sick. Yes! Being on missions is not for the weak.

I only had one weet-bix for breakfast and I then made a positive decision to go and spend time with my DADDY. HE took me through six Psalms from *PSALM 22 till PSALM 27*. I felt much better after that knowing that my DADDY cares about me. I told Simáo about my stomach and proceeded to ask him about getting the church roof fixed in position. He had a few tasks to do and said he would join me later. While waiting for him I carried on with the children's Jungle-Jim.

It was 11:45am when Simáo came to see what was needed with the roof and after seeing what it was I was busy with, he realised we needed help from the children to get the roof sheets up on the rafters. Simáo had decided to ask the children to sacrifice their afternoon school so that we could get the roof completed by that evening. There was a new buzz of excitement as Simáo spoke to the children when they arrived there a half hour later. They realised that there was a need and that they could fulfil that need. Fernando and Domingos got up on to the rafters with Simáo and I. Simáo then asked the children to bring the sheets up one by one. When the roof sheets started coming up we could place it and make sure that the first row was correctly placed so that the others could follow on as we nailed them down row by row. Simáo had nailed one of the corners so that it would be easier to place the other sheets in position as required by us. The roof sheets were coming up row by row but the wrong way around. The two boys and I had to turn the sheets around on the roof and only then place it in position. We on the roof were standing on the purlins with an open roof under our feet making it awkward to turn the sheets around as we had to do extra balancing to enable the turning to go smoothly. This was no easy feat, we were at risk of one slip and you fall to the ground below injuring yourself badly.

I realised that it would be much better and safer if the sheets were turned around on the ground and then passed on to us. I spoke to Simáo but he was not very interested because he was nailing the sheets in position, this was a much easier task. Realising that the supervision of the roof sheets needed to be done immediately as we did not have a lot of time left, I started organising the children in groups of four so that the job would not be so taxing on the children. All wanted to help but it was only the bigger ones who could help. The groups of four were divided into two boys and two girls as I realised they would be better balanced for strength than four boys and four girls each.

To my amazement and what turned out to be utter despair each and every sheet had to be turned around which was still fine, but the despair was the children on the ground had to be told to turn every sheet as they brought it to us. There must have been between forty to fifty sheets to be turned before lifting it up. I have no further comment on the roof saga "frustration" but praise be to GOD all the sheets were nailed on and not one broke. The rest of the children realised they were done and all of them disappeared.

There were five of us left standing inside the building and we looked at each other with great big smiles of satisfaction, Simáo, Dinho, Fernando, Domingos and myself. I got all of us to stand in a circle holding hands and to start praising and thanking GOD for giving us the endurance, the ability, the patience and the strength to complete up to that stage, what was a mammoth task. After that we proceeded to bless the building for what was still to happen inside that building. HALLELUJAH! PRAISE THE LORD! All that was still needed was to get the sides closed up. We packed up and the boys went to have supper with the rest of the children and Simáo and I went to the mission house to have supper and tell them the good news.

CHAPTER 25

THE PAPER MACHÉ FRAMES AND LAYING ON OF HANDS
FRIDAY 20 AUGUST

This morning was a good morning for me. I was feeling a thousand times better then yesterday. It was 6:30am and the anxiety I felt before I went to sleep was completely gone, PRAISE THE LORD! For he is good, He is good, He is good, HALLELUJAH! I got into my regular morning routine and then had breakfast.

Ntombi was up early this morning because she had something she wanted to ask me to do. I was on my way to my room to finish my breakfast and then have quiet time with my DADDY when she said that there was something she would like to show me. But when she realized that I never started work without having quiet time, she was quite willing to wait till I was done.

Well this morning I was not sure which direction I should take with my quiet time. I asked the HOLY SPIRIT for direction, and the answer came immediately. The direction was left to me, it was my choice. How honoured I felt and took the direction to the Book of *REVELATIONS, Chapters 19, 20, 21 and 22*. I thoroughly enjoyed being present in the GLORY of the LORD as these four chapters so splendidly portrayed.

It was good and wonderful to see how GOD`S Great Holiness with Compassion and most of all HIS Love as well as the New Jerusalem was to come in all its splendour. The awesomeness of the size of this fantastic city was in magnitude too much to comprehend. The size being 1500 cubic miles which when looked at was about the square size of South Africa at the base and then the same size in height and in width. All glory to you LORD.

I went to see Ntombi where she took me to the bungalow which was being used to make paper mache or paper pulp or whichever way you wanted to describe this product. I preferred using paper mache as it was laid out on frames with wire gauze stretched tightly across it. The women doing this would then take one or two of the many field flowers growing in the area around the bungalows, and place it strategically so that it would enhance the already natural fibre and vegetation used to make the paper mache.

These wooden frames were made by the carpenter who built the bungalows on the premises. Ntombi wanted me to see how I could fix two of the frames as they were starting to come apart. She took me to another bungalow where there was plenty of wood and quite a number of doors and window frames for additional bungalows, stored. I took what I thought would be enough wood for six more frames. We then went to the church building as it was close to the generator room in case I needed to use the electric drilling machine.

The frames had all been assembled with nails and not screws and because of the moisture in the paper mache, the wood had started swelling and caused the nails to rust and the frames would come loose. I removed all the nails and replaced them with screws. The frames had immediately become rigid. Now because of the nails which could not hold the wood together as tightly as the screws, the gauze wire became slack and had to be re-stretched. When the frames were fixed and the gauze wire re-stretched, I could then cut the wood for the new frames. As I finished this operation Ntombi arrived with a slice of cake and a cup of coffee. It was a very welcome site and the look on her face when she saw the frames, made my day. I carried on working until lunch was called and carried on after lunch until I needed the generator round about 4:00pm.

The generator would not start. I had to report it to Ntombi as it would be needed for the night's electricity at 6:00pm. She told us to let it stand for an hour as it was most probably flooded. It was by now 5:15pm when Domingos and Dinho tried starting it again, still nothing happened and as we looked at the generate I saw petrol leaking out the exhaust pipe. Somehow petrol had seeped into this pipe from one of the petrol pipes.

I proceeded to dry the exhaust pipe and generally drying the whole motor. We watched all the joints and clamps and saw that there were no more leaks. I also replaced the rope which was used to turn the main pulley to start up the motor. Well after the boys and I had repeatedly tried to start the motor, it gave a few puffs and slowly but surely it started running smoothly. Domingos refitted the exhaust pipe with new screws as the old ones were very rusted. Everyone was happy and we left it running as it was already 6:15pm and the light was fading fast.

Ntombi soon called for supper as she was preparing supper when I disturbed her with the generator. There was a gas stove in the kitchen so that if anything should happen with the generator it would not matter. We had supper and Ntombi told me that Amelia and herself were not feeling too well, especially Amelia. I laid hands on Amelia and Ntombi praying that the LORD`S stripes HE bore on HIS back would do the trick for them.

Here I do not use the word trick as if some form of magic must take place. No, here I used that word as an analogy just to show how quickly the LORD`S healing takes place when we believe. Yes, It does not matter where you are or under what circumstances we find ourselves in, it is our belief that we will be healed by the laying on of hands that brings the healing by faith. While I was praying, Rachel and Mama Katerina, one of the adult women on the premises, stretched out their hands towards them in agreement to what I was praying. AMEN!

After supper it was back to my journal and off course bedtime. I thanked the LORD for the day and tucked myself in my sleeping bag and I did not know when I fell asleep.

CHAPTER 26

PHONING THERESA MY WIFE
FRIDAY 21 AUGUST

I got up at 6:00am and had to rush to the bathroom. When I came back I went straight into bed and fell fast asleep again. I woke up with a start at 6:50am when I heard a vehicle pulling into our yard. I got up and went straight to the house and found that Ntombi had been up already. The visitor was inside talking to her.

I entered and was introduced to the visitor, whose name was Dieter. He had been sleeping in his vehicle somewhere in the bush for nights and was glad when I offered him coffee. They knew each other but not very well. We chatted for a while and about 8:00am he left.

When Simáo is not at home, I always feel that it is my responsibility to take care of the home and everyone living on the premises. This is the reason why I moved so quickly to see what was happening. When Simáo leaves on his weekend trip the look between me and him tells it all. *"Look after Ntombi and my people."* It is enough for me to take the responsibility. When Dieter had left I went to do my morning routine and had breakfast after that.

This morning in my quiet time I thought I was onto a good thing with the 2nd coming of JESUS, but something was bothering me. There was a nagging urge to phone my dearest wife Theresa. I asked Ntombi and used their landline to phone Kuilsriver, Cape Town, South Africa where I live. Her cheerful voice told me that she was glad to hear from me. Twenty Five days had now gone by and I was also longing after her.

She phoned back and we had quite a long conversation. All was well at home but they were asking when I would be coming home. Our conversation eventually turned towards "The feast of tabernacles". This is a feast that our church "Lighthouse Christian Centre" celebrates every year since our senior pastor got this vision from GOD to hold this feast celebration, as the Bible states, every year.

Theresa told me that this year's feast was all about the "Nations". She also told me that the dear sister in charge of the feast decorations, Tannie Issy, was waiting for me. I had become one of the team members who decorates the church at this September/October time at the church. There was also work to be done at the "Children's Church Production". I also spoke to my son Jaime. It was good to hear his voice and I asked him about the well-being of the dogs at home. We said our goodbyes and I felt good and that I could go on for the rest of the month to come. I decided to complete the frames Ntombi needed before lunch. We had a very nice relaxed lunch as it was Saturday and we all decided to take it easy.

After lunch I carried on with the completion of my project, closing all the gaps along the edge of the roof in between the rafters. When I was done there I carried on with the children's playground. The last two rungs still had to be added to the second ladder which was the second of the main supports. These two supports would be used for the children to reach the top and the in between levels of the Jungle-Jim. The four horizontal poles which were to be used to join up the two ladder supports had jagged ends which had to be squared up.

By now it was 4:00pm and I felt thirsty and a little peckish. My walk on the pathway leading from the church took me straight to the kitchen where I had a lovely cup of rooibos tea and some biscuits. After tea Ntombi asked the children to help me carry the two ladders and the rest of the poles to an area lower down from where we were and also away from the buildings.

Ntombi and I agreed that the children needed to have an area of their own without having to worry about making noise or disturbing the bungalow area. The area chosen was well placed as it was just a few metres away from a huge tree which one could see had been there for many years. The branches were so thick that the children could tie ropes with a tyre tied at the loose end of the rope. To give you an indication of how huge in bulk and not so much in height this tree is, I can vouch and say that the branches being used for their swings were as thick as our trees growing in and around our cities and surrounding areas back home.These trees do not grow very high as I stated earlier, but its size lies in the spread of its leaves and its thick trunk which can support the thick branches I described. A magnificent bulk tree with its huge plumage spread across the top of its main trunk.

When we travelled on the sandy gravel roads, we saw these huge trees standing singly out in the veld areas away from the bushy areas. After examining the ground in the immediate vicinity around this huge tree, I chose what I felt to be the ideal spot. Dinho and his friend were only too eager to dig the holes for the two ladder supports. While they were digging I nailed the poles together and when I was done we all packed up as it was getting dark. At the ablution building I took a light splash washing the day's dust from my upper body and then went to fill in my journal. I managed to lie down for a short while before supper was called.

When I entered the house to my surprise Augusta had arrived back from Maputo where she had gone for her motor bike driving test. She did not have a pleasant experience needless to say, but I will not expand or make comment. We sat around after supper enjoying a cup of coffee and biscuits. Then in one movement we all got up, greeted each other with a hug and off to bed we went.

CHAPTER 27

MY LAST WEEK AT "IGREJA COMMUNITARIA de MOÇAMBIQUE" SUNDAY 22 AUGUST

AUGUSTA`S MESSAGE

I got up at 6:30 am and did my regular routine. What a beautiful morning! The wind had been blowing very strong the past two days and nights. Today was the first windless day and it was good. There was a thin layer of clouds high above and the temperature was just right. I could walk around early morning in a sweater with me breathing in the beautiful fresh air. I had breakfast and then had quiet time with my DADDY who ministered and uplifted me, making me feel so good. Before preparing for morning service, I washed my clothes and then asked GOD to bless the morning speaker and all those attending. Service this morning was to be in my partly completed project. The roof was completed but the walls still had to be completed.

Augusta was to be in attendance at the service. Mamma Katerina led the worship as worship leader although there was no title. She was faithful, A very humble person and dedicated in what she had to do. Augusta`s message was straight to the point. Her message did leave a few people shifting around in their seats. The message was from the book of *DANIEL CHAPER* 3.

Her message was about Daniel and his two friends where the three of them were in the burning furnace with the angel. Daniel and his friends were faithful in worshipping GOD under all and through all circumstances and GOD protected them while they were in the furnace. She further broadened her message by preaching and talking into their lives.

"Do not worship idols, spirits, ancestors or any other GODS, but rather walk in GOD`S blessings by worshipping GOD and Him alone."

After service I took a photo of all the children in front of the church`s open door and then relaxed a little while waiting for lunch. As we finished our lunch Ntombi arrived back from Malangwani, a few kilometres from there where she had preached to people in the area. I went to lie down till 3:00pm and decided to go to the beach. To my surprise I found that Ntombi, Rocha and some of the children were already on the beach enjoying the lovely afternoon and the gentle waves as they washed up on the smooth sand.

I joined them at the water's edge and started walking in the opposite direction I walked last week. Further down there were some interesting rock formations which seemed to have sprung up there from out of nowhere. There were no other rock formations anywhere near these formations. Normally one would find one or two other rock formations close by, but here was nothing. I did not swim but walked in the water ankle deep. It was very refreshing while watching a crab scuttle across the rocks and me picking up the odd shell as I walked along. I had such peace and could think about many things including Theresa and Jaime at home. As I turned round some distance from the rocks I saw Ntombi and the children had packed up and had started walking up the steep loose sandy hill towards the sand and brush track which was occasionally used as a road.

There was a group of boys still in the water swimming around naked. They had walked down to the beach with me. One of the three dogs on the premises followed us and was romping around in the water. As I approached them I called them as I did not want to leave them there alone. The group of boys, there had been five of them, were very bashful when they saw me looking at them. They had never been naked in front of me or anybody else other than their own people. I turned around away from them and walked to the bottom of the sandy hill to wait for them so as not to embarrass them any further. They ran across to where they had left their clothes laughing and when they caught up with me as I slowly walked up the hill, they were still laughing.

I started running up the hill and they gave chase, catching me half-way up. We all had I good laugh and walked from there soon catching up with Ntombi and the other children. The dog came running to us with his tail wagging. I felt so good and accepted here at the orphanage, even the dog, I never got to know his name, came to walk next to me.

We walked over to where I had erected the main structure of the "Jungle-Jim" and had a good look at what I had erected. Ntombi felt it was inadequate as she thought I had finished. I first listened to her as she made suggestions to add to the structure and then proceeded to let her know what I had in mind for the next day, which was Monday.

We both agreed with each other's suggestions because it coincided with the whole concept. Here was another aspect of GODS input into this whole idea. There was one other thing she wanted me to do. Rocha being only two years old and two other children not too much older, would not be able to walk across the horizontal poles as they were a bit too wide for them and also they were too young. I saw what she was saying and I then also decided to make a small ladder which could reach the bottom horizontal poles.

The off-cut wood which I could collect from the church building could be used as a walkway across so that the three young children could also enjoy this facility. While we were discussing the younger children the others were already climbing up and down the two ladders and the bigger ones straddling the horizontal poles as we agreed on the additional wood.

We then went on to the big tree and saw where the four swings could be suspended from the four thick branches. It was only the fourth swing where I would have to cut away a thinner broken branch which broke when the boys tried to hang the rope swing from this branch because access to this branch at the time, had been easier than the others.

I went to wash the beach sand and sea water off my legs and feet and a few minutes later Rachel came to call me to supper. After supper I had fellowship with the women until 9:30pm and greeted them and went to bed.

CHAPTER 28

FERNANDO AND ME
MONDAY 23 AUGUST

I got up at 6:00am. The air was a bit misty. We were expecting visitors from Maputo today. After my regular thing, I had breakfast and then quiet time with my DADDY. Oh! How HE loves me.

I started out early with the Jungle-Jim. Simáo and Ntombi did not have a good night's rest as Rocha got sick during the night. They were going to take him to hospital in the morning. Ntombi eventually went alone as Simáo had to wait for the visitors. Only two of them arrived. They were going to do some teaching that night and show the "JESUS" film the next night.

The children helped me carry the big ladder that I made while working on the church building, down to the big tree. We then went back to fetch the rest of the poles we found on the premises. We managed to use as many poles as was still needed. There were two poles left which I could place strategically as balancing bars.

I felt it was a good strong structure, sturdy and solid in spite of there not being any rocks around to support the main poles in the ground. Two of the boys wanted to help knock in the nails in the boards forming the walkway. The two boys, they have to learn at some stage of their lives, could not knock in the 50mm nails I was using because of the hardness of the poles cut from the trees in the area. It needed a strong sturdy arm and accurate hard hitting. I told them that it was alright when I saw the disappointment on their faces. They so much wanted to impress me. Domingos came down to help me for the last hour. He was a big help. Ntombi and Rocha came down from the house and was very impressed with what she saw. She left to get the supper going and Domingos and I finished up at 5:30pm.

When I came to the house Ntombi asked me to check and see how I can temporary set up the lights in the church. Fernando helped me to rig up the wiring and the plugs. When we switched on the main plug, the lights would not go on. Fernando, after I asked him if he had switched the plug on, his answer was "yes" with a grin. I opened and checked the wiring on the three plugs on the lead. There was nothing wrong with the wiring which was securely fixed.

I then went over to the bungalow where the lead was plugged in to see whether there were any loose wires. When we arrived at the bungalow as we entered the door, first me, I saw what I saw, and then he came in and saw what I saw. There was a table standing under the plug where different types of work were done. Now comes the realization, the plug was lying on the table and as he, Fernando said, the wall plug was switched on, but the plug on the lead was lying on the table, not plugged in.

Fernando looked at me with a big sheepish grin on his face. He knew I had wasted my time opening up the three plugs attached to the lead. I pressed the plug in the wall and switched the plug on and voila! The two globes were burning lighting up the whole church. Again he looked sheepishly at me while this *beeeg* grin came on his face. I could not help myself as I also started grinning and then we both started laughing.

We grabbed each other hugging and as we walked out we were still walking with each other's arms around each other's shoulder. There was such an understanding between myself and the three boys who helped me with the church that whoever made a mistake we would not hold it against that person.

Moments like these makes for better understanding and having more tolerance towards one another. We are all human beings striving to do our best so that in the end we should all care about one another. Do not hurt each other's feelings, do not look down on another person's weaknesses, do not ridicule anybody, but show love and understanding as the dear LORD would show it towards you. Most of these children have no fatherly relationships with their father. Some of them do not even know their fathers. Be a father to the fatherless as GOD is a FATHER to all.

Ralph W.J. Sedras

We had supper as our guests joined us with a very blessed fellowship amongst us around the table. After supper we went across to the church for the service. It was a very blessed service with the children singing and dancing as they led the praise and worship. The message was good although I did not understand much as it was in Portuguese. I could feel the presence of the HOLY SPIRIT. After service we went back to the house for coffee and then to sleep.

CHAPTER 29

REALITY- THE SOBERING EFFECT
TUESDAY 24 AUGUST

I got up at 6:15am with the air again a little misty. My regular morning stint was done with and breakfast did not take too long. As always, the time I make to take a positive decision to have quiet time with my DADDY before I start my daily work, was well spent with him.

At the Jungle-Jim, the post holding the rope to be used for hand over hand swinging was coming loose. I went to look around and after about an hour I came back with three fairly large stones which I could knock into smaller pieces and put it in the hole around the base of the pole. Also I could nail a few pieces of wood as stays across the bottom length in the hole.

These stones and sand together with the slanting stays cut from the top of the poles did the trick. After that I got stuck into the two swings and got everything ready and then had lunch.

Here I have to go back to Monday 23 August which totally slipped my mind while writing my journal. Ntombi took us to one of the families in the area. It was a nice walk, about 5 kilometres away. Our group consisted of the two guys from Maputo, Ntombi, Rocha and I. We found the family at home except for the man of the house. The walk to this family and being there with them was very sobering to one's mind.

To see two women and two children, two little girls, just sitting cross legged on the ground doing nothing, staring into nothing, just blank expressions of utter despair, was pitiful. Man, people I tell you, you just have not seen or experienced such poverty until you have been on a mission's trip. We need to get out of our comfort zones where we are so content and satisfied that we are going to be with OUR FATHER one day and do not have to worry about anything or anybody else. Yes, you have made provision; you have worked hard for it, so why must you be worried. Shocking, the way I have expressed myself? Yes, maybe but it is exactly the way it is supposed to be, the reality. It hit us all like a bolt of lightning.

One excuse why we cannot go on such a trip is often: "I am not by the means" or "GOD has not revealed to me that I should go". Another one sometimes used is: "I`m a sender not a goer". As they say in Afrikaans "Dis 'n flou ekskuus", or in English, "It's a lame excuse". Some may say "Who does he think he is!" Yes, as I stated, it is meant to give someone a wakeup call.

Whatever your "excuse" is, GOD is not interested in your excuses, why should HE be when HE has already started using someone else who is obedient when HE speaks. Here is a softer take on what I just said. Your input into the trip can be so huge and awesome just by praying or having a share in cost of sending the one person who is obedient when GOD speaks. You might genuinely not be able to go but am by the means to help with the cost, yes help those who are willing to go. Please I gently ask, do not stay in your nice warm comfort zone.

My thoughts came back to where we found ourselves as the man of the house came home from fishing out in the nearby lake with nothing to show but two long sugar canes he managed to find growing along the dirt track. Ntombi and the one guy spoke to the family and he also brought a short message. Ntombi asked me to pray a blessing on this family and I also prayed for GOD to bring healing as I could see the hurt from being so poverty stricken, almost destitute.

What was so sad for me was that they had chickens, quite a number of them running around. The family was staying in their bamboo and bull-rush huts where the ground had been pecked so clean and bare by those chickens that they could not lay eggs. But here was a big but; the people did not want to slaughter the chickens because the chickens had to lay eggs to supplement the meagre food supply they had. Another sad aspect of this situation was that the chickens could not lay eggs because there was no food, not even a crumb to eat. I learned later that at least once a week, sometimes twice a week, one of the chickens would lay at least one egg.

Man I tell you, we think we are poor when we erect a make-shift shack for shelter for a home and have to depend on finding a piece of scrap cardboard or scrap metal or yes, even an empty beer bottle to sell at the scrap yard.

"We ain't seen nothin' yet". There is no cardboard, no metal, no bottles, yes, no nothing to sell. If by chance a passing vehicle travelling by would drop a piece of cardboard or angle iron piece that one could take to a scrap yard, it would be luxury items. These items would be of no use to them as there are no scrap yards. People thank GOD that here at home you can still sell some old newspapers for cash as these will be used for recycling.

We walked back to where we were staying not one of us saying a word to each other, each of us with our own thoughts just moving our feet forward. Even Ntombi was visibly shocked when we came across this family.

The two Portuguese ladies made lunch for us on our arrival but I must tell you I did not enjoy what I ate after witnessing what I saw. For me the lunch we were having was a luxury. Ntombi had left them a bag of flour and a few items she thought this family might need. She had it in a backpack which I carried on my back as Rocha was carried on her back by Ntombi.

After lunch I left with Augusta and the two guys to another little settlement, where we found Mama Gogo. She was a weathered old lady who was really ageing fast with her best years behind her. The two guys, I never got to remember their names, were both brothers in CHRIST. The taller of the two guys talked to the old lady and he proceeded to pray for her. Augusta had to translate for her as she could not understand him. We left there and on the way home I asked Augusta whether we could walk past the school. It was break time when we arrived there and after being introduced to the principal and one of the teachers I asked him if I could take a photo of him standing with the children. The school consisted of two classrooms with the children sitting on the floor. The principal had a table and a chair which he used. The other lady teacher was not present as she had taken the day off.

We left there and walked on home. Once we arrived we got the lead going again and they plugged their lead into ours because the area they were using for the "JESUS film" was quite a few metres from the power source. It really is amazing how news travels here. There are no cell phones or landline phones that one could send a quick message or make a call. All communications still happens by spreading the message by word of mouth from one person walking to his settlement and then one of them would walk to the next settlement and let them know.

The "JESUS film" is based on *"the Gospel of Luke"* and translated with a narrator`s voice coming over loud and clear above the two speakers playing some music. It was a blessed evening with me being able to follow the film, as I know *"the Gospel of Luke"*. We had a good day and night, very blessed by what we had seen and experienced. I went to sleep after helping with the packing up of equipment and disconnecting the power.

CHAPTER 30

THE VISITORS
WEDNESDAY 25 AUGUST

I got up at 6:00am because all the adults had been asked to go to the church for Morning Prayer before breakfast. We had a blessed morning centred on faith. The scripture was from *"LUKE" CHAPTER 7 FROM VERSE 3 TO VERSE 6*. These verses were about having faith in GOD when HE sends you to go. It does not matter where it is HE sends you as long as you go having faith and trusting HIM. It is for us to be obedient because GOD will be moving on using the next person who is willing to go.

Why must we sit here and wait to die? Let's rather get up from our comfort zone or from the place where you feel you just have not got the strength or the will power to move forward trusting the LORD.

Yes get up and do something that is beneficial to not just one person but to many people. Not to say that because you have been beneficial only to one person and your friend or brother in CHRIST has been beneficial to more than one or even a room full of people, that you are less blessed than your friend. No, THE ANGELS OF THE LORD REJOICES when one soul comes to meet JESUS to accept HIM as that person's personal saviour.

The WORD says that it is better to be obedient than to offer up a sacrifice. The blessings that follow you will be so awesome that you just want to run with them. We had breakfast and the two brothers in the LORD left at 10:00am. Simáo, in the meantime had left for Durban at 9:30am.

I got my tools and went down to the playground and worked there all day. There was a problem with the other two swings that still had to be hung. It just was not easy as I thought it would be. The clamps were the main problem. They could not go through the chains. They had to be ground or filed thinner with a hand file. I was there for the rest of the day until supper time. Patience was my main practise while I was filing those clamps. I had to file a little and then see if it will work, then file some more until eventually it would go through. We had supper and I was straight to bed after that.

CHAPTER 31

THE ROPE LADDER
THURSDAY 26 AUGUST

Rising for me this morning was a little later at 6:25am and after doing my regular thing I had breakfast and then quiet time with my DADDY. Now came the making of the rope ladder. Firstly all the tools and equipment that Simáo had accumulated over the years are stored in a bungalow made of a wooden frame and covered with reeds, which he calls "the Tool Shed." The rope, the chain, the seats and brackets had all been stored in this building when they bought it at a hardware store in Durban about two months earlier. It was now only the rope that was still left in the shed.

I got the rope out and went to the church building where there were quite a number of pieces of off-cut wood from the cutting of the new slope of the church roof. These off-cuts were packed neatly to one side. I took 15 pieces with me as I did not know how many I was going to use. Two of the younger boys were with me. They helped me and were also around me just to see what I was doing. Yes, these children had enquiring minds just like any other child growing up in the city.

I worked out a size visually with one piece of wood lying flat on the ground and me standing on it making marks on either side of me visualizing the action of a child climbing up one step at a time to reach the top. I measured 300mm between each step and laid the rope out on the ground and also placed the steps next to the rope at each 300mm gap. I took ten steps which made the ladder about 3 metres long. After finding a suitable drill bit for the 2 holes on each piece of wood, we went over to the generate and I checked to make sure that our petrol supply was enough as Simáo had not arrived back from Durban yet.

Here we unfortunately have to check for petrol first before using any power tools, whereas at home we plug the power tool in the wall plug and switch it on and "Bob's your uncle!" This is part of the difficulty of being in the missions' field. He had left the day before with the motor bike to fetch the bakkie as the mechanical work on the bakkie had been completed and it was ready at the Toyota agents in Durban. Here in the mission field one has to check everything you use so that there can be no malfunction of one or more other activity which could be affected because of one malfunction, or shortage.

Once the holes had all been marked equi-distant on all ten steps, the actual drilling of the holes did not take long. I used the jig-saw to cut all the steps to the same size. The rope ladder was taking shape. The rope had to be laced through all the holes like shoe laces. I made a knot at the end of the rope which I then laced through and pulled the knot hard up against the wood which would be the underside and also pulled the knot as tightly as possible. The reason for the knots to be very tight was so that the steps would not go skew which would make climbing up the ladder very difficult.

After that another knot is made above the step and also pulled as tight as possible so that the two knots will act as a lock where the rope goes through the hole. This prevents any up or down movements making for a very stable step. I had 300mm marks on the floor of the church and knotting and adjusting the knots on the floor became easier the more knots I made until I eventually came to the tenth step.

The other side had to be made in the exact same manner. The adjusting of the tension between the two holes and getting the 300mm space between the steps was the difficult part in this whole operation. When one sees a rope ladder being used as a rescue ladder being dropped from a helicopter or even down a mountain side one does not realize all the work involved in the making of a rope ladder.

After lunch Ntombi, Augusta and Rachel with some of the bigger children went on a walking visit. The two boys were still with me and helped me carry the assembled rope ladder down to the big tree. Once we were there they helped me put the big wooden ladder which we used at the church building, up against a higher branch than the highest branch used for the swings.

I threw the loose ends of the rope over the branch and proceeded to tie it at the top around the branch at what I felt was the correct level for the bottom step. This step was just high enough so that one has to climb up from the ground and then only stand on that step feeling the balance of the ladder as it moves around before being steadied by the weight of the person standing on it.

One of the boys in his eagerness to see how it worked climbed on the bottom step and started climbing up. I had to stop him as the knot was not as tight as it should be causing the rope to slip. I had to go up the ladder to re-adjust the knot again and ensure that the knot was tight enough and not slip again.

When I had finally finished after cutting the excess rope I found that the length of rope left was long enough for another rope ladder. I did not make another rope ladder as we had decided that the one ladder was enough. The left over rope was to be stored in the tool shed should it be needed for whatever reason. I stepped back and looked at the whole set-up and thanked GOD that the children`s playground was finally finished.

I put as much detail as I could into the making and erecting of the ladder so that whoever reads this book can use the information for their benefits where ever it is needed also other operations and repair jobs that one has to do in any situation. *"The WORD says that what we learn or experience over the years or period of time, we should not hold back on or teach as the day will come when the LORD calls you to rest. Of what use is it to anybody if all the knowledge one has gained goes down the grave with you."*

There are those out there who say "I had to learn the hard way why must I give all my knowledge to you. You can learn and look out for yourself." This is such a wrong attitude of self and does not benefit anybody. Have an attitude of giving to others what you have received, knowledge, so that all can benefit. Life generally will be so much easier and more understanding for the next person because of your unselfish giving. Bless those who come behind you by leaving a legacy. Amen! There was now one other job to be done; the making and mounting of shelves in the building used as an office. This bungalow consisted of two rooms of which the one room was bigger than the other. This room had been used as a classroom before the new and bigger school building on the hill was built. The smaller room contained books, art materials, paper and items pertaining to the development of the children. There were also Leggo Blocks, Jig-Saw Puzzles and some Toys donated as missionaries or passers-by saw the need of the children.

They could not store all these books and equipment any other way than in boxes stacked on one another. This way of storing and packing was not good at all. When they needed a particular item, in most cases they had to remove two or more boxes to find what they were looking for. Somewhere during the time I spent on the church building and the swings I had managed to erect a shelf on the inside wall of the bungalow I lived in. Ntombi had seen this when she came into the bungalow and realized that the problem they have in the office could be solved by making two rows of shelves on two of the walls. She had asked me and the time had now come to get the shelving up.

I gathered all the wood I needed and Ntombi showed me exactly where I should mount the shelves. The wood I needed came from off-cuts of the new slope of the church roof. I measured the height and distance between the shelves. It was getting dark by this time and also Ntombi and the others had come back just after 4:00pm.

Supper was soon called; Simáo had not come from Durban yet. Ntombi was a bit worried as he should have been back already. We had just finished supper and Ntombi was busy talking to me about the paper they were making when we heard the bakkie's familiar hooter some distance away.

We were both glad and surmised that there must have been a delay in Durban. Two minutes later we heard the bakkie stop next to the house in the driveway. There had been a delay in Durban, but a very good one. The back of the bakkie was fully loaded with chairs and foodstuffs. The missionary, Derek, from Durban had arranged that the church he belonged to should donate twenty plastic chairs to "Igreja Communitaria de Moçambique" so that everyone could at least sit on a chair in the church. These twenty and the other chairs in the building just about filled the church. Praise THE LORD!

Derek had also arranged with a bakery near the church to instead of throwing away all there expiry dated breads, rolls, and cakes and whatever the owner felt he did not want anymore, to put it all in black bags and he would distribute it to the poor in the area. Well with Simáo in the area and the poverty on the premises, he gave the two black bags to Simáo. Simáo had now arrived there with this load and the rest of the supplies needed at the orphanage. All the bigger children came to help unload the bakkie and while they were busy, I said goodnight and went to fill in my journal which I must admit I had neglected to fill in for the past two nights. Simáo had re-assured me that the boys could manage the unloading. I went to sleep after that, tired but satisfied.

CHAPTER 32

RAIN AND BECOMING A GRANDFATHER
FRIDAY 27 AUGUST

I got up only at 7:40am. It had been thundering and raining all night. It was heavy thunder rolling from one side of the sky and right across to the other side, accompanied with heavy downpours. If it had not been for the toilet calling me, I would have stayed in bed much longer. When I came out of the bathroom and got dressed, I left straight for the kitchen.

I met everyone there having breakfast. After greeting them I made my breakfast and went to my bungalow to have my breakfast in the presence of my DADDY. I had another wonderful time. Well after that I dawdled about and chatted with Simáo. He could not get hold of pastor Manzini as his cell phone was switched off. He left a message for him to phone back.

I carried on with the two shelves in the office until lunch. Just before lunch was called I asked Ntombi whether she would take a photo of Dinho, Fernando, Domingos and I at the church building. Together we did the alteration to the church building with me working all day and the three of them joining me in the afternoon after school.

After lunch it was back to the shelves. Dinho helped me and was of great assistance so that I could complete all the shelves by 5:15pm. I went to check for any leakage on the roof and found the church floor completely dry. There were no leaks in spite of the heavy downpour during the night. I reported back to Ntombi and while we were talking it started raining very hard. She suggested that I check the roof for leaks while the rain was falling so hard.

I went back when it slackened and looked up at the underside of the roof sheets. I could see that there was moisture by some of the old holes where the water had seeped through. Ntombi said that the bitumen used to seal those holes had been sent to Katwaan. Simáo had gone to Manguzi to buy some petrol and was supposed to find out what time the bus would leave on Tuesday to Johannesburg. Simáo had slipped up and apologized for not being able to tell me. He immediately phoned pastor Manzini, but his cell phone was again switched off and he had to leave a message.

Supper time was upon us and it was here that Ntombi asked whether I knew someone called Olivia, as she had given birth to a son. The caller had not left his or her name but I knew who it was from. The call had to have come from "Liefie", (Lovie) as I affectionately call my wife, to let me know that I was a grandfather. Yes, Olivia, my daughter had been due to give birth while I was in Moçambique. And so it happened that on Thursday 26 August 2004 at 2:30pm in the afternoon, I became a grandfather. It made me feel good and I thanked GOD that mother and son were fine. When I went to bed a little later we were still not sure of the departure time of the bus to Johannesburg.

CHAPTER 33

THE BIRTHDAY
SATURDAY 28 AUGUST

I got up at 6:45am and did my regular thing. The weather was fine with some cloud about but no rain. I had breakfast and then quiet time with my DADDY. It was a good and encouraging time for me as Simáo had disappointed me by not finding out the correct time and day of departure at Manguzi. It was the second time in three days he had been there and still did not find out. As I am writing this, I realise that his mind must have been occupied with other things like supplies and equipment.

I was preparing my breakfast when Ntombi told me after speaking to Kobus who brought me across the border, that he would not be able to help us because he is in Empangeni till Sunday. Ntombi had been phoning around the previous night to enquire about the transport and had also asked Simáo to come home that night and not Sunday as he normally did. There was a bus from Manguzi at 4:00pm that Sunday afternoon. I then asked Ntombi if there was anything she still needed me to do as this was my last day here.

She requested one last task. There was one A4 frame to be made and another had to be reinforced at the corners. Outside lying across the tarred poles was a sheet of galvanised sheeting. I cut the four corners of this sheet and used these corners to reinforce the loose frame. This whole operation took longer than what I thought it would.

I had to cut the wood strips to the correct thickness with mitred corners. I had to make sure that all cutting and drilling got done at the same time so that the petrol in the generator would not be wasted. With normal electricity it is so much easier to do one step at a time. Out here we all have to think of saving to avoid a shortage down the line. There was no lavish splashing of resources at all. One soon has to learn on a mission trip.

Lunch was called. It was a light-hearted fun lunch. It was only Ntombi and I who were fully versed in English. I won't elaborate on what happened at lunch as there were two Portuguese ladies and two Moçambican men at lunch. We all had a good time.

After lunch I went back to the frames. I finally completed them at 5:15pm. What a job it was. After chatting to Ntombi about the paper, I got the two boys to help me carry all the tools to the workshop and generally tidy up and clean up where I worked. After a light splash I went to lie down until lighting up time which was at 6:15pm managing to fill in my journal before supper was called.

Today was also one of the little girls' birthday. Her name was Linda and she was three years old. Augusta had made a fridge cake and placed three match sticks as substitute candles on it. I thought that was a brilliant idea. After prayer with the children, the matches were lit and we sang the "happy birthday" song to her and each of us had a piece of cake. Everyone was happy but the biggest smile came from little Linda. Yes even at the orphanage we have time out with each child so that they can all feel special. It is very sad when one looks at the situation at "Igreja" and realizes that most of the children here did not know any other way of living a normal life other than living out here without parents.

For them Simáo and Ntombi become there adopted parents, Daddy and Mommy. There have been cases where more than one child had been found wandering around in the bush crying from hunger and fear of the unknown. They have no idea what the word "Family" means or is. At the most none of them has ever had a consoling word from a parent or a loving arm around them. Never have they as a child walked alongside there Daddy feeling the safety and comfort of holding the hand of theirFather walking bravely next to him thinking in their childlike mind "This is my Father, my Daddy, I feel safe holding his hand."

Yes!, the tragedy of all of this is the child being told to stand just there where he or she is and that his or her Daddy is going to see or go behind that tree over there. An hour, two hours pass by, the child too young to understand what is happening until they realize when it starts to get dark that Daddy as he has done in the past will not be coming back. Oh! Yes!, Then they were at home at least in a place of safety.

What now, they were in the area unknown to them, not familiar with and do not know anybody here. With fear now fully having hold of them, they start calling out and soon the first tear begins to roll down their cheek and soon into a full and fearful cry. It gets so dark out here in the bush, in the jungle that they might soon not be able to see anything so they find a hollow in the ground or a tree stump to sleep in or next to for shelter.

Out back home generally at night, there is a starlit sky or a bright moon and if not the street light or the house lights itself. Yes, you out there back home, Mothers and Fathers do not neglect or abuse your children. GOD has chosen you to be their parents, Mother and Father. It does not matter under what circumstance your child or children have been born, GOD chose you to be their parents. It may not be as easy as it seems but just as it is difficult for me to write this message it is what GOD had laid on my heart.

Bring your children up in the fear for the LORD as far you can, with you being their role model. Yes! *"May the LORD bless you and let his face shine upon you in all that you do. May your basket always be full and your going out and coming in always be blessed and your borders always be increasing."* GOD be with you!

Do not be the cause of your child or children stumbling for the WORD says that you might as well tie a millstone around your neck and jump in the sea. Be the proud parents of your children as you and they grow and develop together.

This insert was "HOLY SPIRIT" led and I thought it would be appreciated as it is the LORD`S desire that we as parents can be blessed and proud of our children. As *PSALM 127 and 128* says *"We as parents should be able to sit around the table with your family, your children and shoot them out as arrows from your hand into the world."* We should not be embarrassed to release them into the world. Ask GOD for direction and guidance for your children. AMEN!

I phoned my Liefie in Cape Town to let her know of the new arrangement. I counted paper and envelopes with Ntombi and found a congratulations card and envelope for Olivia and her new baby in Cape Town. We both went to sleep after that, me in my bungalow and Ntombi with Rocha her son.

CHAPTER 34

THE MOMENT IN MY LIFE I WOULD NEVER FORGET
SUNDAY 29 AUGUST

I got up at 6:40am. The weather was good. "GOD is good all the time, and all the time God is good." After getting myself all splashed up, I had quiet time with my DADDY and then breakfast. The next thing I had to get on with was packing of my bags and getting all my things together. I also had to accommodate all the extras I had accumulated during this month.

I had to cut the packing up short as it was time for church. There were a few minutes to spare. I decided to go down to the playground and there pray a blessing on everything I had built and that there would only be fun and laughter and no injuries. There were 4 swings, 2 rope ladders and a Jungle-Jim with accessories. I left there with apprehension of how the children were going to enjoy themselves and was off to church.

The church was quite full with lots more adults and youths present. There were also a couple of visitors including a visiting speaker from the Bible school in Maputu who had been with Simáo in Katwaan.

Mama Katerina conducted the first part of the service. She was a very quiet and humble person in spirit and commanded great respect from everyone present. The children sang and soon all the adults joined in. Following this, groups of 4 to 5 were formed and rendered singing and dancing items which were also well received and very blessed. Tithes and offering time was handled well by Augusta. She was interpreting for me as Ntombi had gone to Gwala by motorbike (Suzuki) to preach there.

I was given an opportunity to thank the children and everyone else who had been involved during the month I had been here at "Igreja Communitaria." All this had been pre-arranged without me knowing. What a pleasant surprise and blessing. This Sunday morning had been very well arranged as Amelia, one of the two Portuguese missionaries got each child to draw a picture of how they saw me or how they experienced me there amongst them. They had all been given an "A5" size page and drew as they felt and expressed themselves accordingly. Some of them drew pictures, others wrote thank you messages in broken English.

Amelia and Rachel had assembled all the pages into an "A5" book with punched holes laced together with a neat Portuguese patterned ribbon tied in a bow. This was a presentation carefully thought about and carried out with Love to me in thankfulness for what I had been and become to them, "Uncle Ralph." I had been sent there to them to be a light amongst them.

This was a moment in my life that I would never forget. It really moved me strongly to think that what the LORD had planned for me had actually happened by HIS grace and was so blessed beyond what I would ever have imagined.

Here now I am not being boastful or proud but thankful that I was so obedient when my wonderful DADDY spoke to me through HIS HOLY SPIRIT, HALLELLUYAH!. The children danced and sang a special song for me. After this whole blessed event I waited to see what was next on the agenda.

It was time for the sermon which was to be held by a man named Julius. He was this particular Sunday's speaker. The message was very blessed where the first part was a testimony by him of how the LORD saved his life. He was a happy go lucky worldly, drinking man not knowing what it was to be sober. He realized that he could not go on living like this. That was his first step away from where he was headed. We all have to come to that point in our lives where the realization of the road we are on is a no go road, which leads you ultimately to your total downfall. He did not testify of exactly what happened or how the LORD had turned his life around. But today wherever he went, he sings the LORD'S praises testifying and talking about his new life in JESUS.

His message was from *EZEKIEL chapter 3 from verse 19 to 20.* We who knew JESUS must warn and disciple our lost brothers and sisters when you know there is something happening in that person's life that is not right. The WORD says it becomes your responsibility to be a watchman and to be vigilant about that person's life. You have to warn and speak to the guilty person or persons not in a judgemental way but in love so that the person you are speaking to can realize that what you are stating is being done purely and sincerely out of love and concern for that persons well-being.

For me it was a sobering message making me realize why it is that GOD places us all in various strategic positions. After service lunch was prepared while I completed my packing. Ntombi soon came home and then we all had lunch together. This was to be my last lunch together with my Moçambique family. Then came the anxious wait for Simáo from Katwaan. This wait was not so pleasant. He eventually pulled up there with some of the children who could still go home to their parents or parent in their homes.

The bakkie had been swept and the canopy still had to be fitted. I then fitted the canopy with the help of a few of the boys. Dinho was busy siphoning petrol for the generator as the bakkie was loaded with some goods and especially my luggage. We finally left me happy that I was finally on my way home, but sadly looking at the children running next to the bakkie shouting and waving as Simáo drove slowly away. The goodbyes to everyone had gone off well as if I was going down the road and coming back again. Yes, I was coming back again, but only the LORD knew when.

Simáo drove on a road that I have not been on yet. He said that it was a shortcut and would take us ahead of a very bad stretch of road. This shortcut helped us reach the border at 3:40pm. When we left there ten minutes later 3:50pm we were still some 20 kilometres away from the bus.

Fortunately from there on the road was tarred all the way. We were now in South Africa and across the border. We were rushing to get to the bus by 4:00pm. When we checked the time again it was 3:58pm and we were still some distance away. Two speed bumps did not help any as we were now slowed down by pedestrians along the road as well. As we arrived the bus started leaving for Johannesburg. Simáo stopped right in front of the bus not allowing it to move another centimetre enabling me not to miss the bus.

The bus driver got out to see why Simáo had stopped in front of the bus. After Simáo had explained what my predicament was, the bus driver saw Simáo's desperate act as the only way out. He allowed me to board the bus after opening the luggage compartment beneath the seating in the bus to load my luggage.

We said our goodbyes, Ntombi, Simáo and me hugging each other in a threesome, not one of us wanting to look the other in the eye. The bus left Johannesburg and Simáo and Ntombi carried on to Durban for they were headed in that direction. The bus trip was uneventful. A couple of crude toilet stops alongside of the road in the bush and two longer stops further on. The stop at Pongolo was an hour and a half long. I felt it was far too long but the other stop at Ermelo was only fifteen minutes. I managed to sleep most of the way when it started getting dark. We arrived at Johannesburg Park Station at 3:30am.

I could refresh myself in peace without having to look out for my luggage all the time. At the Greyhound bus reservation office I waited on a bench nearby and when they opened at 5:30am, I was their first customer. This was a blessing as I went across to the reservations and explained to them that I had missed my return date. To my surprise I was told that it was off season and that the ticket dropped from R410 to R345. I received R65 back in cash. What a blessing with me not having a cent on me. There was a bus leaving for Cape Town at 1:00pm. HALLELLUYAH!

I tried to find my Bible Bag which I had lost on the up trip but was unable after one of the reservation attendants had made enquires. I resigned myself to a lost cause and boarded the bus at 1:00pm. The journey back home was very tedious and tiresome as I was anxious to get home. After a bit of site seeing from the bus before it got dark, I slept most of the night. The bus arrived in Bellville at 8:00am and I waited about half an hour before my son, Craig, arrived with his car. My wife Theresa and both my sons, Craig and Jaime were there to welcome me back home. What a blessed trip I had, safe and blessed knowing that what GOD had planned HE had fulfilled through me. I give GOD all the Glory and Honour for HE is good and faithful and loves us all. HALLELLUYAH! AMEN!

THE END

The Poem Inspired and Composed by Amelia in Portuguese
with the English translation by Renato below:

BRING THE LIGHT

IN THIS DARK WORLD
WE ARE THE LIGHT
SURE HOPE ARE WE
HOW WILL THEY KNOW
THAT CHRIST LOVES THEM
AND HAD DIED TO SAVE THEM

BRING THE LIGHT!
BRING THE LIGHT!
THE LITTLE CHILDREN SAY
THAT GOD GREATLY LOVES YOU
BRING THE LIGHT!
BRING THE LIGHT!
TELL THE WHOLE WORLD
TILL THE NIGHT LEAVES
IN THE NAME OF "JESUS"
BRING THE LIGHT!

COUNT UP THE MILLIONS
BOUND BY SIN
DYING ON THE INSIDE
HOW WILL THEY KNOW
THAT CHRIST LOVES THEM
AND DIED TO SAVE THEM

YES! GO TO THE WHOLE WORLD
IN THE NAME OF "JESUS"
BRING THE LIGHT!

EPILOGUE

I had taken numerous pictures of work in progress and everything else around me including the various operations on the premises. My biggest disappointment after my exciting stay in Moçambique was when I opened my camera to send the spool away to have it developed. The film had not wound up inside the camera, the spool had slipped off the little winder sprocket and was lying folded in layers of film.

I have gone back to Moçambique every year since this trip in 2004.

The new house is a blessing from GOD for their faithfulness in living and being obedient in the purpose that they had been called to, in that area of Moçambique.

Amelia had written a prophetic poem for me in Portuguese. It took four years before this poem was translated into English. Thank you my "bro", Renato for this translation!

Now here was another case of practising your faith and putting your trust in GOD. Renato was born in Brazil where their language is Portuguese. He had been living in South Africa since the age of twelve. At the time of this translation in 2008 we, Renato and I had decided to go back to Moçambique for two weeks, this was truly a trip of faith.

Renato had been unemployed and was not sure where his next salary would come from as he had just been retrenched. Together we went into prayer before GOD. GOD`S answer showed both of us that he must come with me and voila! the translation came about from this trip.

Do not trust GOD for things you know you can get, but rather trust HIM when HE speaks to you and sends you knowing that you have a need. Missions are about being obedient to GOD when HE speaks to you and then having faith and trusting GOD knowing that HE will supply your needs, Halleluyah!

Renato had an interview to fill a vacancy for employment on a full time basis just before he left on this trip with me. At the time he was not sure whether this vacancy would still be available when he came back home but the vacancy was still there waiting to be filled by none other than "Renato". PRAISE THE LORD!

BE BLESSED AND KNOW THAT GOD LOVES YOU!
AMEN! TO GOD BE THE GLORY!